Diaries of a Casual Worker

Bev Wilkinson

Copyright © 2020 Bev Wilkinson

ISBN
978-0-6486593-2-7 (paperback)
978-0-6486593-3-4 (ebook)

All rights are reserved. No part of this publication may be reproduced, stored or transmitted in any form, or by any means (electronic, mechanical, photocopying, recording or otherwise) without prior written permission from the author. Enquires should be made through the publisher.

Some names of people and workplaces have been changed to protect identities.

Cover Design: Malvolio Pty Ltd
Layout and typesetting: Busybird Publishing, www.busybird.com.au

A CIP catalogue record for this book is available from the National Library of Australia.

Contents

Dedications	I
Acknowledgments	III
About	V
The Confession	1
My First Proper Jobs	5
Wearing the Purple Uniform	7
Embarking on My First Adventure	11
Camp Catacombs	15
Theme Park Goals	20
Relatives and Factory Life	21
Paris	25
Ski Season	28
Dreamworld Life	32
Study	36
Casual Work on the G.C.	38
Back Home to Melbourne	42
Events Industry	44
Volunteering at Business Chicks	50
The Seeds of a Business Idea	55
The Beginning of Celebrate Living History	58
Networking Drama	63
The Dream of Travelling the World	67
Back to Studies	74
The Full-Time Job	78
Side Gig as an Activity Coordinator	84

Lift Off of the Forget About Ages Tour	87
New York	90
North Carolina	96
Chicago	99
Milwaukee	101
Atlanta	106
New Zealand	110
Horse Racing Jobs	113
Recruitment Agency Work	115
Home and Community Care	120
Call Centre Life	124
Working During Coronavirus - Public Transport	129
Working During Coronavirus	132
Impact of Coronavirus	134
Processing Life	137
Post-Covid Public Transport	140
The Second Wave	142
Entrepreneurs: Generations Apart	144

Dedications

This book is dedicated to all the people that dream big, but are scared to take the first step toward making that dream happen. I hope this book inspires people to take a chance on themselves, and just go out and give their dream a go. We only live once, so we might as well try.

Thank you to my parents, Nerisa and Bob Wilkinson, and of course my furry mascot, Ava Dognar.

Thanks to my good friends who cheered me on! Thank you Frida Soerensen, Melissa Haber, Kate Hart, Gail Dudeck, Bruce Petrie, Celeste Milano, Skye Reilly, Edie May, Russell Morgan, Cecile Laffan, Mandy Hay, Chris Bolding, Rebecca Crothers, Su Jo Lee and Belinda Gates.

Sarah McLennan from Malvolio Pty Ltd, thank you for supporting my huge ideas over the years. You helped make the ideas in my head a reality.

All my supporters at my casual workplaces, and of course my Celebrate Living History crew, you are my cheer squad.

Acknowledgments

Thank you to all the workplaces that have given me an opportunity to be an employee. Without taking that chance on me, this book would not have been possible.

I am so grateful to have been employed in many industries, and this diversity has made me into the person I am today.

At the time of writing this book, I was still employed by some of the workplaces mentioned. For that I am thankful.

I hope my book inspires others to pursue casual work as a stepping-stone to making their dreams a reality, and to making friendships that may span years.

I have so many fond memories related to my casual jobs that make me smile every day.

All profits raised from the book will go towards publishing costs and funding not-for-profit Celebrate Living History, an organisation established with the focus of documenting stories and forming connections between young people and seniors. And of course, producing stories that make you smile.

To view some of Celebrate Living History's stories by our wonderful interns, visit www.celebratelivinghistory.com

Bev Wilkinson

Founder of Celebrate Living History, and casual worker

www.celebratelivinghistory.com
facebook.com/celebratelivinghistory
instagram.com/celebratelivinghistory

About

Diaries of a Casual Worker features the real stories of the working life of Bev Wilkinson who, as a creative person, has had to find ways to fund all the amazing dreams in her head.

Bev has been working in the casual workforce for over 10 years and she has loved the diversity of the many industries she has been in. These jobs not only fund her creative passions, but have formed an important part of her world.

As a child, she never really knew what she wanted to be, but she always knew she wanted to be creative. She had big dreams and loved to write and draw. As an adult, she still loved to write and draw but realised she couldn't make a living doing what she loved.

Like a beacon, casual work came into her life and she realised there was a way. She could still do what she wanted, but she just had to rely on other roles to fund her dreams.

Her journey into the casual work world began, where she formed many friendships and enjoyed the diversity of the many roles that took her on. Her personality rose to the challenge and she thrived in many industries, including event management, call centres, aged care, disability care and even ride operating. She has always been in multiple positions, and at times forgets where she is meant to be!

In her spare time, she hatched big dreams and was confident she could make these ideas in her head, a reality. She did not have to rely on grants. She relied on her ability to work more hours, to hire the people that could make these big dreams a reality.

Bev, while juggling all these casual roles, went on to create Celebrate Living History: an internship program formed to connect generations through storytelling. Forged through her work at nursing homes, she could see the potential of connecting young and old. Bev felt sad seeing those at the nursing home without any family. In her eyes, that disconnection could be made so much better if that older person had a chance to share their story with a younger person. She loved it when the residents had family over. The residents' demeanour changed, and, in a sense, a spark of joy reignited. A simple connection can change the entire world for one person.

While working in her casual roles, days off and evenings were dedicated to mentoring young journalism students to interview and write stories on seniors in their community. Just working with the students made Bev happy, and she felt like her purpose in life was coming to light.

She loved education, and working in casual roles provided the means to make that happen. She also went on to create *Entrepreneurs: Generations Apart:* a book created out of her curiosity of what makes business owners, aged under 30 and over 60, embark on making their dreams, to live doing what they love, a reality.

Through her work diaries, she hopes to inspire others to just go out there and make their dreams a reality. You can make it happen, you've just got to find your own way to make it a reality.

Chapter 1
The Confession

Lesson: Have pride in your appearance and try your very best.

Hi there! My name is Bev Wilkinson, and I have a confession to make. I'm a casual worker and I'm proud of every job that I've done! And that's saying something, I've been in so many diverse industries!

Some people frown down at casual work, as it is not permanent. You don't have any paid sick leave and you can be fired with short notice. Casual work is not secure, your hours can vary depending on the demands of the business. And that can be quite scary if you have big responsibilities like a mortgage, family, or a dog that loves the good life.

But for me, I love the casual workplace and without having jobs in this environment, I would have no work to support my creative side. I am grateful for all the employers that have had faith in me over the past few years, and I am appreciative of the many opportunities these employers have given me to grow as a person.

Having flexible work schedules has allowed me to pursue my creative passions and do what my heart aches to do: write, and mentor young students. I love sharing my knowledge and not having to worry about income coming in. I can be free to do as I please and just say *yes* to making my dreams a reality.

When I tell people that I usually juggle many jobs, the most common reaction is, 'Why?' For me, I have always enjoyed being busy and having a role in life. I love the little things, like dressing up. Joining the everyday world and having a purpose. Just getting up and knowing what the day holds for me. Relying on just one income stream scares me, and to be honest, I always feel secure having back up jobs. If I lose one job, that's fine, I will still have income flowing in to pursue my creative side.

I have learnt so much from being in the casual workplace for over 10 years, and I'm looking forward to sharing my journey with you.

In these 10 years, I have become a uniform hoarder. If you had a peek in my wardrobe, you would see some of my greatest outfits. My stash of colourful uniforms represents many different industries. They range from bright yellow to purple. I can't part with some of my uniforms, for some reason. They represent a point in my life that makes me smile. I think of the friendships I've formed and the memories I've made, wearing these uniforms.

A simple uniform not only represents the company you are working for, but the pride you have within yourself. I always have a sense of joy putting on a uniform. It sounds corny, but I love being in an environment where my talents and skills are celebrated as part of a team. And a simple way of seeing this is the uniform, flagging the colours of my workplace for the day.

Some people know exactly what they want to be at a young age, but to tell you the truth, I had no clue.

I was envious of those who knew exactly what they wanted to be. I remember watching an episode of *Futurama* when Phillip J. Fry received a career chip, he had no choice. His role in life was to be a pizza boy, and that was that. I was envious that decision was made for him. But in the real world, we have to make the decisions. Who do I want to be, and how can I make that a reality? That's the beauty of having choice, but then again, if choice was streamlined to one industry, such as being a pizza boy, life would be much easier. And you would not need so many uniforms!

When I was at school, it was difficult to choose a career path. How, at such a young age, would I know which path was good for me? There was a scary time that I decided to study accounting simply because my friend was in the class. I didn't even like maths, yet here I was in this class that celebrated numerals. What was I thinking? I didn't pass the class, instead of studying I ended up drawing pictures in the margins of my books.

I always did love creativity and did well in art class. That was a time where I could really let my imagination flow. I remember going on to a field trip to a museum in the city. It was so much fun. I was left alone with my notebook, and I was transfixed, looking at some of the intricate costumes from all over the world. I gazed and lovingly sketched down the details of the costumes. My teachers were amazed that within one hour I had created my own masterpiece inspired by these costumes. I look back and wished that I could turn back time and nurture that inner artist and see what she could have become.

There was a stage where I dreamt of being a flight attendant, they always looked so beautiful. I loved how flight attendants were always perfectly made-up. Their makeup was always on point, and their uniforms always well maintained. I loved the scarfs and the red lipstick. Being a flight attendant looked so glamourous, especially being paid to travel the world!

I wanted to be part of that glamourous world, and as a child I would make believe that I was on a plane serving customers in the playground. I pretended that I was serving gourmet meals and that everyone wanted a cup of tea.

But reality soon struck when I grew up and discovered I was too short to reach the overhead lockers. I was devastated, but still wanted to be a part of the tourism industry, so I enrolled in a Diploma of Tourism. I wanted to be on the other side, booking dream holidays for people to fly on these magnificent airplanes.

After graduating, I realised that I hated using the online booking system Galileo, which was necessary for booking these holidays, then once again my dream of working in the tourism industry was dashed!

I was destined for life in the casual job world, where my path would be like going down a rabbit hole, never really knowing what fate awaited me.

Chapter 2
My First Proper Jobs
Lesson: Have fun find a job that cherishes your personality.

My first job was working in a chocolate factory when I was 16. At the time I thought it was pretty cool, I could feel like *Charlie and the Chocolate Factory* and have so much fun. This job turned out to be the opposite, the days were long and repetitive. I wrapped the same products over and over again. I didn't have anyone to talk to and I was getting pretty bored. I lasted a week during the school holidays and decided the job was not for me.

My second proper job was working in a pizza store as a kitchen hand. I wasn't very good in the kitchen, and got in trouble a few times for stirring ingredients. I loved walking to the counter and talking to customers with the front of house staff. That's the area I thrived better in, I simply loved having a good chat and escaping the heat of the kitchen.

I lasted two weeks before I was fired. The manager decided I wasn't a good fit for the business. I wasn't too sad to be leaving to tell you the truth, the kitchen was hard to navigate, and I preferred talking to customers.

Pretty early, I realised my personality was not suited to this type of back of house role, and I was totally fine with that.

Luckily for me, an opportunity to work at the newly renovated theme park in Melbourne, Luna Park, arose. It was the year 2000, and I spotted an unusual job posting on Seek.com. It was to be a ride operator at a major theme park in St Kilda. This job looked amazing and I wanted to do something that suited my personality better.

I applied for the job, and a few weeks later I was offered an opportunity to be interviewed. I remember at the time I was so stressed about what to wear. I found a professional looking jacket at the back of my wardrobe and a fancy white top that I wore to my formal, and paired these with a black skirt.

I looked at the mirror and I felt like a proper professional person, ready for the group and one-on-one interviews.

When I arrived at the hotel where the interview was being held, I felt a weird sense of butterflies, like I knew I was on the cusp of getting my first tourism-related job. I entered the room and put on a big smile as I greeted the person at reception.

I was faking being confident when really, inside I was sweating and screaming, *Get this over and done with.*

On reflection, I had nothing to be worried about. I tend to put big barriers up when all I need to do is relax.

I entered the room, and I saw the other people being interviewed smile, and just enjoy the company of the people they had just met.

This set the scene for an interview like none I had ever experienced before.

I had so much fun. We played games and I laughed so much. It was very refreshing to not feel too much pressure, and to just let go and let my personality shine through.

It took a week to find out the verdict of the interview. I was so anxious to find out if I was successful. I remember when I received the call that I was successful in joining the Luna Park crew, I was jumping up and down it felt like I won the Lotto. Finally, a job in the tourism industry that was fun and suited my personality. I could not wait to wear the purple and yellow uniform and to operate rides for hundreds of people from around the world. I may not be flying to exotic destinations every day, but I was surrounded by people from all different countries and I didn't have to leave Melbourne!

Chapter 3
Wearing the Purple Uniform
**Lesson: You never know what opportunities arise.
Wear bright purple and smile.**

I stayed at Luna Park for four years. I was so proud to be wearing that purple and yellow uniform, even though my white t-shirt sleeves were often coated in grease from the rides I operated.

I will always have fond memories of my time at Luna Park. One of my favourite moments was the first Christmas party held at Luna Park in 2001. The Christmas party was magical. We all wore masquerade outfits and it felt very glamourous having the park opened just for us staff to enjoy.

Our supervisor, Daniel, treated us like we were absolute stars and he drove the Scenic Railway around the park just for us. I loved the wind in my hair and screaming through the tunnel as we travelled, enjoying the night view of St Kilda. I am always amazed to think that the Scenic Railway has provided so much joy for many people since 1912 when the ride first opened, and that I was one of the many passengers of the Scenic Railway.

We also enjoyed photos with the heritage-listed horses on the famous Carousel, which was manufactured by the Philadelphia Toboggan Company in 1913. It was amazing to think that many generations got to experience this simple joy over many years.

I also remember meeting Delta Goodrem who, at the time, played Nina on Neighbours. She was so sweet and down to earth, taking the time to hang with staff and pose for photos.

At the time, my favourite show was The Secret Life of Us, which was an Australian television drama set in St Kilda. I absolutely loved that show, and when I heard they were filming at Luna

Park when I wasn't working, I just had to come in. I felt like a huge stalker, but it was worth it to have photos taken with Deborah Mailman who played Kelly. I felt like a schoolgirl who wanted to scream, Oh my god, I met Kelly! It was so cool to watch a scene being filmed in person, and to see my favourite characters in person.

Sometimes I enjoyed being on the cleaning roster, as it was an opportunity to just wander the park and chat to people. But when I heard over the radio, It's a code rainbow, I wanted to run away! Code rainbow meant vomit; I never knew how gross it was going to be until I rocked up to the ride. I remember one of the rides was closed for hours as we had to soak the vomit in kitty litter and hose down the little bits of fairy floss that were stuck on the insides of the seats. I'm not sure why, but in nearly every vomit, I would spot flakes of carrot, too! This job was definitely not for the fainthearted! I remember telling myself that I wasn't cleaning vomit, it was really dried up biscuits!

Sometimes people steal the most random things, such as the tops of the taps in the ladies' toilet. One strange item that was stolen was a radio that we used to communicate to each other. The person had stolen the radio and was ranting random codes into the speaker. My team leader had to play detective and tried to find the culprits. It turned out they were at McDonalds across the road! Of course, they needed a meal after a hard day of crime!

I never thought Luna Park would set the scene for a marriage proposal. It was so sweet, the customer made a request to stop the Sky Rider, which is the giant Ferris wheel, at the very top. It was the perfect night for a question that would affect his life forever. The views of the ocean were beautiful, and you could see the twinkling lights of the city. In a few minutes, the Sky Rider stopped, where he made awkward conversation. He took a deep breath and seized the moment. The night was warm and balmy, and ready to welcome this one huge question. With the carriage swinging slightly, he took the ring out of his pocket. He gave his girlfriend a slight smile and asked the magic words, 'Will you marry me?'

She loudly said, 'Yes!' She could not stop the smile on her face. She was over the moon, finally she was going to be married to her best friend, forever. I will always be in awe of how one theme park can spark memories that will last a lifetime.

Luna Park was also the place where many staff relationships bloomed. Some of these relationships are still together today. I remember one staff member had wedding photos on the Carousel. She looked so beautiful and happy to sit astride a horse with her newly married husband, where they spent many hours together. It was amazing that a workplace could connect people who otherwise would never have met. This couple went on to create a life together, and now have one big, happy family.

What I loved about Luna Park was when we finished work, we all went down to the local pub and enjoyed a few drinks. It was so fun to chill and talk about the day. We were such a huge loud group, and you always knew when the Luna Park crew were out on the town. Often some staff members would still wear the purple and yellow pants with flair.

I always enjoyed these outings. In a way, it felt like I was part of a huge family.

Our social life was at the park, so we needed to play a little bit in the outside world.

I, at the time, had an obsession with Snoopy at McDonalds. If you bought a Happy Meal, you scored a Snoopy. I had a Snoopy for all occasions, and would often bring Snoopy as a mascot to our trips to the beach and pub. One time, we were all enjoying drinks and Dave Hughes, a famous comedian, came into the bar. I was pretty drunk and felt brave, so I asked Dave to pose with the Snoopy and I. He laughed but obliged. I think he thought I was a little bit crazy. Not many people would ask him to pose with Snoopy, that's for sure!

I absolutely loved late summer nights. We would all walk down to the beach and enjoy a few drinks over a game of cricket. Watching the sun set over St Kilda beach was truly a beautiful sight, and it was a bonus that I could spend some of these moments with my Luna Park family.

I'm still in touch with many of the people that I worked with at Luna Park, and I am so grateful for these wonderful friendships that have evolved over time. We shared so many moments together, particularly through working double shifts! These lasted from 11 am to 11 pm. The hours were long, but we bonded together through our love of working on rides. It sounds silly, but this was the time my mind could explore, through my imagination. One of the rides, AS1, which was a space simulator, left you free to daydream once you buckled in the passengers and put the ride in motion. The pilot was Michael Jackson, who navigated the universe with his passengers, yelling, 'Saber one to Saber three. Danger! Dang, I'm gonna get you.' While waiting for the 5 minutes to end, I was left on the platform, thinking about the cute little mouse that lived near the ride. I wondered where the mouse lived, and if he had a little mouse family. As you can tell, my mind is my own amusement park. I like to think of random things to keep my mind active. Sometimes, when you do a job that can be so repetitive, it's the only way you can keep a smile on your face. I'm happy in my own make-believe world. Why focus on the negative, when you can make a colourful world of your own?

It was working at Luna Park that provided the skills to travel to the United States as a go-cart instructor.

Every day, I operated the dodgem cars, helping customers become unstuck and providing helpful instructions such as, 'Turn the wheel', to people of all ages.

It sounds simple, but combined with language barriers or too much enthusiasm, often I would receive blank faces when I yelled out the instructions.

I learnt to be patient and to work well with young children. I had a few tears when children would get too rough bumping each other. Sometimes children would get too competitive and forget being on the dodgem cars is meant to be fun, not a race until the end.

Chapter 4
Embarking on My First Adventure

Lesson: Be patient. Sometimes all we need to do is relax and great things will happen.

All throughout my life, I saw the United States as being an exciting destination full of culture and life. I loved the old Hollywood movies and have always had an admiration for Walt Disney. I have enjoyed his animations since I was little girl and I wanted to set foot into his amusement parks, where dreams can come true. A way to get paid, and travel the United States, was the camp counsellor program which I had heard about while I was studying. This program sounded amazing, I just had to sign up to an agency and they will do the work finding a camp that suited my skills and abilities. I could be placed in any camp around the United States, and that was pretty cool. I would experience life as a local and meet other camp counsellors from around the world.

I had been to the United States previously with my family, but this journey was so different. I was on my own, and had succeeded in saving the funds to make this happen while working at Luna Park. I was proud that all my efforts would result in this one trip of a lifetime to the other side of the world. Looking back, I remember it was a long process to be offered a position as a camp counsellor. I did not have highly sought-after skills, such as experience being a Lifesaver, but I was full of enthusiasm and had worked with children from all over the world. I had also got an amazing reference from my supervisor at Luna Park. Surely that would be enough?

I remember calling the camp counsellor program office constantly to see if I was placed. I was feeling very anxious and worried that I would not be offered a position, and even at some stage thought about pulling out. I had high hopes, and after a few months my patience was rewarded. I was finally offered a position as a go-cart and minibike instructor at Camp Catacombs in Connecticut, and set about making my dream trip to the USA a reality.

I purchased my round-the-world ticket and pinched myself, I was really going on my first overseas adventure solo. Just me and a suitcase, with the world at my feet.

I remember being so nervous leaving Melbourne Airport for the first time. I was worried about not having someone to depend on, and it just being me. But I was also excited to explore another country and meet new people. I was at the point where I was pretty nervous. I visited the airport bathrooms so many times, even when I did not need to go!

I was also in such pain. I was so silly, the day prior I thought to save the inconvenience of having to shave my legs while travelling, so I would try to wax my legs. Big mistake! I ended up having painful blisters on my legs. It was ok, but I needed to make sure that I tended to my legs with lots of Aloe Vera during the flight. One huge tip, if you are planning on travelling, do not do anything drastically different before you leave!

Luckily, my friend Liz took my mum and I to the airport. I remember Liz blaring up these cool tunes and saying, 'Listen, this music will pave the way for many unique memories.' Every time one of these songs play now, it makes me smile the biggest smile, as I remember the time I embarked on my first solo trip.

I have always loved being at airports, there is something about seeing planes flying off the tarmac that I love. I often wondered where the planes were going and how long it would take to get to the final destination.

Now it was my time to board a plane, and I was so excited to have scored a window seat. I love to look down from the skies and feel like a bird, so free. The fluffy white clouds and the little specks of human life buzzing on the ground.

No matter how many times I fly on an airplane, a simple flight makes me feel like a small speck in the universe, it really grounds me and makes me realise that no matter what my problems are, in the whole scheme of things it doesn't matter. I'm just a small cog in the world. I just need to shake it off and do my own thing. I am my own person and I will do the best I can do.

On our way to Los Angeles, we stopped over at Auckland, where I bumped into a few others who were also in the camp counsellor program. It was great to stretch our legs and have a chat before we had to board the 14-hour journey to Los Angeles.

When we touched down at the Los Angeles airport, it felt so surreal. I could not quite believe that I was finally in America. I felt like a zombie, jet-lagged, but managed to find the camp program shuttle that would take me to the camp counsellor induction venue.

I was so grateful that we had a few hours to sleep at the hotel, and then make our way to the conference venue for induction. Even though I had those few hours, I still felt out of whack. But was eager to learn more about the role that I had embarked on a journey to the other side of the world for. I quickly made so many new friends. We all bonded together simply because we were Australians with a bad case of jet lag!

All my new friends were excited to explore the USA and I was happy to have people to travel Los Angeles with. Just being in a big group made me feel safe and I was so excited to be going to Disneyland with them.

While travelling on the bus to Disneyland, it struck me that there were so many homeless people laying on the benches scattered throughout the city. I felt so sorry for these people and realised that I was really lucky, coming from Australia, to have support from the government if we don't have jobs or a roof over our heads.

It was at that moment I realised that America wasn't all that glamourous, and like any country, they have many issues that need to be solved in order to make their country better for their people.

When I eventually got to Disneyland, it was so cool to see the main entrance ticket boxes beckoning me to purchase my pass for the theme park for the day. When I bought the ticket, it felt amazing to walk through the entrance and explore the happiest place on earth. I could see Mickey Mouse and Donald Duck gallivanting through the park, waving to everyone. I could not help but smile. All these cartoon characters had come to life. It was truly a magical place!

I had visited Disneyland with my family when I was a child. I remember wanting so badly to go on the Dumbo ride. My parents took me to the front of the Dumbo ride where I got my height checked and we discovered I was too short to fly with Dumbo. I ended up having the biggest cry. Because of my height, I wasn't able to fly with my favourite Disney character! Many years later, I was determined to make the little girl inside me happy. Much to the amusement of my new friends, I made a beeline for the Dumbo ride. I could see the elephants floating above the ground, soaring through the wind with their cute little hats. Their giant smiles beckoning me. I did not care that I was the oldest person on the ride, I was finally tall enough to soar through the winds with Dumbo. I felt like a co-pilot, flying along with Dumbo, and it was the best experience to soar and giggle. It may have taken years to make this dream a reality, but I did it! Little Bev was happy she had met Dumbo again, and was able to fly the friendly skies with him.

This trip was the first time that I spent in backpacker's accommodation. I stayed at Surf City in Hermosa Beach, which was party central. I had an early flight to New York, but there was no point sleeping, if you tried to sleep you would just get woken up by the noise. Other than the partying, the hostel was in a perfect location, close to the beach.

Chapter 5
Camp Catacombs

Lesson: Be confident. Act like you know what you are doing. You will eventually become an expert!

Trying to board a flight to New York was hectic. I arrived two hours early but still managed to feel anxious going through security. I had to take my belt off my jeans, and was worried that if my jeans fell down, everyone could see my pink underwear!

Eventually, three hours later, I made it to New York, and then from there I made my way to Camp Catacombs. It was such a long journey. When I arrived at camp and saw the American flags out the front, it struck me that I was in another country, and that I'll be here for a few months.

Being at camp was like another world, and I was glad we had a week to adjust and create lesson plans. In a way, I felt like I had imposter syndrome. Even though I had experience working with the dodgems at Luna Park, I had very little experience with go-carts and minibikes. I was so grateful that fellow Aussie, Peter, helped me learn the ropes. I literally faked it until I made it.

It was fun getting to know the other counsellors from around the world, and I remember fondly our first trip to Walmart.

I was so excited to leave camp and explore a random part of the United States! You could tell we were camp counsellors, with all our different accents and the excitement over different American foods and products! I fell in love with Doctor Pepper Lip balm and Lucky Charms cereal.

I was placed with fellow counsellor Becky, and we looked after cabin two, which hosted the youngest children from age 8–10. I was surprised how regulated the sleeping arrangements were.

When we set up the cabin, we disinfected the beds and had to adhere to the state health department standards. All beds had to have hospital corners, which involves tucking the sheets neatly underneath the mattress using overlapping folds.

When the children arrived, what struck me was how mature these young children were. I remember one of my campers, Lesley, at 10 years old, had a boyfriend at the neighbouring boys' camp. She was so in love and thought he was the one for her. In comparison to me at 10, who thought all boys smelt (I still think they do!), when Lesley's boyfriend dumped her, Lesley cried many tears. I almost had to stop myself from smiling when I said, 'It's ok Lesley, there are many fish in the sea. And one day you will find that special boy just for you.' Despite Lesley's maturity, she held this vulnerability which was reflective of a young child, it was beautiful to see. I believe you can only be young once, and you have the rest of your life to be a grown up. It's such a shame to give away that sense of imagination and fun that only a child can have. I'm glad I grew up at a time where I can embrace my imagination and dream big dreams. Everything was possible and you can embrace just being a child. I didn't care if boys noticed me, I just wanted to have fun.

Some of the children did not want to make their beds, as at home they had their nanny or housekeeper do this for them. It was hard to explain to the children at camp that they need to make their own bed, and this was part of the whole camp experience, having the opportunity to become independent and do things on their own. Some of the children were not happy about making their beds, but in time this became part of their everyday routine.

In the evenings, I had to make sure the children were in their pyjamas and in their own bed. Their big reward for being good was 10 minutes of flashlight time, where they could flick through a book or just play with the light on the wall.

I remember my first class vividly. I was so nervous as I did not know what to expect. When the children arrived for their go-cart lesson, they were so excited and very eager to learn. I had to talk about safety rules. From there the fun began, the children got to drive around the track.

I loved running go-cart lessons as the children became my own pit crew, I got them to wave *stop* and *go* signs. The children also assisted with other participants who were struggling with driving the go-carts.

The children were excited to play with the minibikes, so I needed a special lesson from my new friends, David and Jen. I was playing in unfamiliar territory, and needed to find out how to operate a bike safely in order to teach a class. My very first minibike lesson was with the older children, where we took the minibikes to the local oval, it turned out to be so much fun. I even took a group photo in the end to mark my very first lesson. I did end up becoming confident running minibike lessons for the rest of the season.

I loved having Wednesday as my day off. We got to explore the surrounding towns. One of my fondest trips was to Harwinton, which was your typical sleepy American town. I just loved seeing the old houses and exploring the local museum. I enjoyed seeing how community spirit can really bond a small town together. One of our great adventures was a trip to Boston. This came as a big surprise. I was serving breakfast when I was asked if I wanted to join on a trip to Boston. I was so shocked that I nearly spilt milk on the child I was serving breakfast to.

I only had 10 minutes to get ready for this exciting two-hour road trip! When we arrived at Boston, it felt good to be a part of the civilised world once again, even the trashy and corny billboards were welcomed with open arms.

We ended up at Fenway Park, which is such a strong part of American baseball pride. I enjoyed learning about the history of baseball and the Red Sox home field.

I felt so free and silly on this road trip, it was fun to have the freedom to turn around if we saw something intriguing. Such as this shop we passed by, called *Frudent Fanny's*, we just had to take a U-turn and take a photo with the sign!

One the most common issues I had to deal with was homesickness. Just before bedtime, Lesley decided she wanted to go home. Lesley started to pack her things and ignored me while I was trying to chat to her. Lesley finally calmed down when I told her, 'This is only four weeks of your life, then after that you can go home, and everything will be back to normal.' It can be really hard for these children to be away at camp for so long. Lesley was only at camp for four weeks, while others stayed the full duration of eight weeks. Some love camp, others struggle a little bit as they do miss the comforts of home. But they do end up making lifelong friends.

When it was my turn to be Officer of the Day, which was a vital role in getting the campers ready for the day, I had to play the bugle CD, which was trumpet music commonly used during military ceremonies. This music was meant to get campers motivated for a full day ahead.

To be honest, I was half asleep and needed coffee at that time, so I ended up making a huge mistake. I pressed play on the CD player and instead of trumpets, I ended up playing the audiobook, *Yertle the Turtle* by Dr Seuss, to the entire camp on loudspeaker.

Luckily, my friend Stephanie helped me switch over to the bugle music. Even though I looked like I was anxious about doing well, I was giggling on the inside. I wanted to know if Yertle the turtle found a new kingdom he could call his own!

I conducted the flag call, which involved a roll call of all campers, and then getting everyone to salute to the American flag. It felt weird, like I was having an affair with another country. On the inside I wanted to sing the Australian anthem, but instead I was reading off a piece of paper and trying to sing along to the American national anthem.

I was at Camp Catacombs for eight weeks, and I think this was a great period of growth for me. It was the first time I was away from my family in a foreign country. I learned to be patient and to really listen to campers. I didn't love every moment, and at times I felt homesick, but I was grateful that I had the opportunity to really embrace the American culture.

After camp, I was able to travel around the United States for four weeks. One of my greatest moments was travelling with Robyn and Nicole to New York.

Nicole used to work for *The Ricki Lake Show*, and at the time I was a huge fan. Nicole managed to score tickets to see a taping of the show *B-Boys vs. B-Girls*. I was so excited to join the crowd cheering, 'Go Ricki Go Ricki!' It was so cool to be part of the fun of a TV show that I had enjoyed for so long.

There were so many places to visit in the United States, and I made a silent vow to myself that I would once again travel back to the land of opportunity, with a new dream.

Chapter 6
Theme Park Goals

Lesson: Dream Big! Create goals that you can make a reality.

After the United States, I flew over to the United Kingdom. This was where I started a new dream to work at all the theme parks around the world. I had struck up a pen pal relationship with the manager of Drayton Manor, Tim Sandler, over a few months. I had kept him updated on my travelling and he had promised a few weeks of work as a ride operator at Drayton Manor in Staffordshire. Tim had helped with finding accommodation while I was there for the season. Looking back, I was very lucky to have scored some work at Drayton Manor! Not many people get to go to the other side of the world to be a ride operator! I was a pretty crap waitress, so this was my best option!

Soon I was wearing the green uniform and helping to operate the carousel and classic cars. The way they operate at Drayton Manor was a lot different to Luna Park in Melbourne. It was interesting to see how a theme park in another country was run, and I enjoyed getting to know the different rides and seeing how they are operated on an international level. What was different about Drayton Manor was that they had a zoo, I thought it was so cool that you could see monkeys on your time off. Ironically enough, I did end up waitressing at Drayton Manor during the evenings, to earn extra money for my travels afterwards. It was funny, I had to wear a little dicky bow, which is a bow tie, which I never envisioned myself wearing. I turned out to be an ok waitress after all, however I don't think I would make a successful career out of it!

Chapter 7
Relatives and Factory Life
Lesson: Sometimes pain can overcome you. Take small steps. Even one step can make a difference.

After Drayton Manor, I visited my relatives in Colne, which is located in Lancashire, England. Colne is where I was born and the place where my dad grew up as a child. Colne is a small town that brought up memories from when I was a child, when I would visit my Grandmother. I loved the cobblestone pathways and the journey to my Grandmother's home. Even though I was a small child, I still have fond memories of the comfy fire in the loungeroom, where my brother and I would get to choose a biscuit out of the tin. It was such a simple biscuit tin, but it represented my family having quality time together. Sometimes it is the small things that make all the difference.

I remember my Grandmother having problems with her skin. When she took off her stockings, that moment kind of represented snowflakes gradually falling to the ground. I thought it was magical at the time that my Grandmother could generate so much snow! Little did I know, these snowflakes were dead skin, and gene-wise, she passed these snowflakes to me. My mum would help my Grandmother moisturise her skin when she was in pain. Did you know that olive oil is a great moisturiser? My Grandmother used olive oil in abundance and the oil soothed her skin. Having eczema doesn't seem to be a big deal at first, but the skin is your largest organ and when you're very sore, it's so hard to go to work. I've struggled with eczema since I was little, and at times I just had to grin and bear it, even if I felt like an overcooked crab. My eczema is pretty severe, and I am constantly going to the doctors or dermatologist for something that will work long term. I've switched to lactose free and oat milk, and limited my diary intake (which is hard, I love cheese!). Twice a week, I attend Ultraviolet B treatments, which involves a special machine that emits natural sunlight in small doses, which calms down my skin. I'm lucky that I have olive skin, so there is little risk of skin cancer, which has always been a small concern with this type of treatment.

I've tried different moisturisers to calm down my skin, my favourite moisturisers are either QV Intensive Moisturiser or Aveeno, both these creams work well in curing the dryness of my skin.

I wanted to find a way to naturally calm down my skin, and through my best friend Google, I came across a family-owned business founded by nutritionist, Karen Fisher. Her story was very familiar to me, as her personal family history involved eczema, and became the very reason why Skin Friend existed.

I thought, *Why not try some Skin Friend supplements and see if it works on my skin*, so I ordered the PM supplement, which is a blend of calcium, magnesium, glycine and silica. I found since using the PM supplement every evening, my skin has improved, with the bonus of my eyelashes growing in abundance! My dermatologist has suggested getting a HEPA room purifier, which at this stage is working. The air purifier makes the bedroom a safe haven where you are not exposed to allergens while you are sleeping. I find I tend to stop scratching and have a more peaceful sleep. I also spray Bosistos Eucalyptus Aerosol Spray which is lethal to dust mites. My suggestion is if you have eczema to try many products, and eventually one will work for you! Sometimes stress does trigger my eczema too. No matter what I do, an eczema flair up is my body's way of telling me to relax! My skin gets red-raw again, and I have to get medical assistance. Having eczema is an ongoing battle, but I do my best to keep going one step at a time.

So far, the only thing that worked long term was moving to Queensland for a few years. My skin loves the humidity, and was meant for warmer weather! But I don't let the pain stop me from moving forward, life is meant to be lived even if sometimes it's hard to move. You move, even if it takes a while to put clothes on!

I think I get my will to make things happen from my Grandmother. She was in so much pain, but she still got up and looked after her family. She still went outside and enjoyed life. She didn't let pain stop her from living her life.

Looking back, I wished I had the opportunity to know my Grandmother better. I look at photos from her youth, where she looked so happy. I would have loved to discover the stories behind the photos. This is the thought that sparked the seed for an idea that I would embark on in future years.

After England, I was scheduled to fly out to Paris. I was a bit worried about being low on funds, so I decided to visit the local employment office in Burnley and see if there were any casual positions. I didn't have much of a resume. However, I didn't let that deter me! I literally walked in and asked if they had any holiday positions going. I was keen and eager to work. Being born in England meant that I could legally work anywhere in the country.

The employment consultant called up a local factory and within minutes I had a job wrapping local goods. My first shift was Monday, bright and early. It was nice that the factory organised a bus to pick up all their employees. I appreciated the free transport. When I jumped on the bus, it was full of smokers, which came as a shock as I was used to smoking being banned on public transport at home. Even though I didn't like the smoke, I sat down and told myself this moment is only temporary, and afterwards I'll be able to enjoy Paris on a decent budget.

When I arrived at the factory I was shown around and told that I must check out a show in London while I was in England. I was on tight funds, but I still nodded and said I will. I never did see a live London show, but maybe one day when I visit England again, I will.

I felt incredibly lucky and grateful to have the ability to earn my next leg of the journey. By then, my funds were running low and I had to ask for help from my parents to transfer over funding. Surprisingly, while the work was very repetitive, I did make quite a few friends in the lunchroom. It was a nice way to get to know the locals, and made this repetitive job bearable. Sometimes the best parts of a job are the people that you meet, and they make coming back to the job a little better.

Chapter 8
Paris

Lesson: Be kind. You never know what doors can be opened with a simple gesture

After a few weeks working at the factory, I was able to head to Paris, not worried about struggling on a tight budget. It felt so strange being in a country where English was not the first language. I felt a bit silly entering the arrivals terminal of the Charles de Gaulle airport and asking directions to the local train subway. I asked, 'Parlez-vous anglaise?' (do you speak English?) at the customer service desk. She replied, 'Of course', and proceeded to tell me how to get to the subway. It is funny, such a simple sentence had me so anxious, my palms were sweating.

When I finally sat down on the train seat, a sudden sense of calm flooded me, even though I was in a country where English was a second language. Hearing people chat about their day made the experience normal. I just wished I knew what they were saying.

I finally came to the point where I had to switch train lines, I must have looked like such a tourist. I had this huge map and I was muttering to myself, 'Umm, I think I need to catch this train. Oh no, it's not this train? Oh no, I'm so confused, I don't know what to do.'

All of a sudden, a complete stranger comes up from behind me. He coughed and then smiled. He said, 'It looks like you need help.' He proceeded to give me directions and even walked me to the platform. I was amazed at his kindness, just this simple gesture made my day a little bit brighter. Ever since that moment, if I see a person looking confused and looking like they need assistance, I always offer to help. I believe if you are kind to others, the world can become a better place.

When I finally arrived at the backpacker hostel, I felt like I had achieved so much. It may not seem like a huge achievement, but just the act of getting from the airport to the hostel was huge. I had faced language barriers and lots of confusion over the Paris Métro train system.

Being a solo traveller is hard, you don't have a friend to rely on, only yourself. You have to be your own leader and find the help you need to keep going.

It was so nice at my hostel room. I made two Australian friends, Maddie and Derick. We decided to explore the city together and it was good to have company in a city where English was not the first language.

I was so amazed at how beautiful the Eiffel Tower was at night. You could literally walk towards the Eiffel Tower, following the twinkling of lights.

We also explored the Louvre Museum together, and I was so surprised that the famous Mona Lisa was so small in comparison to other artworks. I could see the Mona Lisa by jumping up and down on my tippy toes, she was so popular that I didn't want to push past people to see her up close. Sometimes you've got to choose your battles and I was content to see the Mona Lisa from a distance. The Louvre is so huge that I feel like you could spend days exploring all the artworks. What I loved about the Louvre is the simple celebration of artwork from all around the world in one spot. So much love and passion must have been placed into these artworks for people from around the world to enjoy.

When you visit Paris, you have to be very careful. Despite being the city of love, there are an abundance of pickpockets who are experts at stealing your valuables while you are distracted. Despite protecting my valuables with a money belt, I let my guard down at the hostel. I was hanging with my new friends, Maddie and Derek, in the common area, when some locals came into the hostel asking us if we would like a game of pool. We were having a good time chatting when one of their mates broke into our hostel room, he stole Maddie's camera and some cash from my wallet.

The burglars had a good con going, which involved distracting us so one of them could reach into our jackets to find the room key.

When I found out money was stolen out of my wallet, I felt violated but grateful they didn't take the full wallet. All my ID, credit and debit cards were in that wallet. I would have struggled to get new cards and identity documents in a country where the main language was French. The main lesson I learnt from this experience was to not keep all your important documents in one spot, because if they were to be stolen, this could potentially delay so much. Especially while travelling, you need to have a passport in order to board your flight!

Chapter 9
Ski Season

Lesson: Let go of fear. Go out of your comfort zone

After travelling overseas, I came back home to Melbourne, where I completed a season working in the snow fields of Mt Buller. I had grown to have a love for travel and didn't want to stop, so I thought working in the snow would be something different. I had initially gained a cleaning job at the hotel, where I shared a room with others on working holidays. It was a different way of life, I got up at 5am to start cleaning at 6am. It was a convenient job as I lived at the hotel, so I literally woke up and I was at work. There was good and bad! I felt very much like being in the Big Brother house, every move I made was monitored by cameras. Management knew every move the staff made! Even though I'm not a troublemaker, I did end up breaking the rules. We were not allowed friends into our room, but I thought I would sneak my friend Kate in, to watch *Home and Away* together. The next day I was told off, my actions were caught by the night audit cameras.

I had received my first warning! I felt like a scolded child, and knew this was the beginning to the end of my employment.

It was hard having roommates and having to get up early at 5am for work. One of my roommates, Sarah, had her friends – who worked at the hotel – come over, and I was trying to get some sleep. I sounded like a grumpy grandma when I woke up and said, 'Guys, I do have to get up early, can you move this conversation elsewhere?' Sarah was upset about her fight with her boyfriend, and decided to ignore me and continue drinking with her friends. It makes a difference when you have respectful roommates, and it was awkward while I was trying to sleep and Sarah was carrying on her conversations, as the room was so small. I could hear every detail and I didn't want to know everything about her personal life.

I made many good friends at the hotel, however I was fired in my first two weeks. I wasn't meant to be a cleaner, I could not work fast enough, and I didn't clean the cigarette canisters. But like every other time, I fell back on my feet. My friend Kate gave me a good reference, and soon I was working in the retail store Buller Sports, which suited me more. I found a new place to live where I had more space to enjoy. It was amazing to come from such a restrictive environment to a new home, where I had the freedom to have friends over and just enjoy life. There was a balance between work and life, which was exactly what I needed.

The person that ran the house held a little side business where he charged backpackers a fee to sleep in the loungeroom. At one time, he had 10 people sleeping in the room! There was an actress that stayed with us for a little bit, at the time she played a police officer on *Blue Heelers*. But I will always remember her as the cool chick that I watched *Harry Potter and the Philosopher's Stone* with.

I shared my room with Krystal, and after a day of work, I needed to go into my room to get my asthma inhaler. The asthma inhaler I had on me was on its last puff. I was just about to open the door to my room when I heard these loud noises. It was Krystal and her boyfriend Shane, getting at it like mad rabbits. I didn't know what to do. My asthma inhaler was so close, but I didn't want to see two naked people in the throes of passion. I stood in the loungeroom and debated with myself. I was pacing the room up and down and felt so anxious, I really did not want to see my housemate buck naked, mounted on her boyfriend.

But my throat was starting to wheeze, and I knew I needed medical assistance. My only relief was my puffer beyond the doors. My health was important, and I had to face this awkward moment to steady my breathing. I decided in the end to push through the door, it made such a loud creak. I used my hand to block my face and turned my back so I could not see anything. It was such a small room, and it was hard to be discreet. In what felt like the longest moment, I yelled, 'Sorry', and ran awkwardly towards the side table where my spare puffer was. I was glad my spare puffer was not knocked off the table in amongst all the passion! Krystal and Shane were not expecting me, and I could hear them jump mid-bonk, and giggle. I covered my eyes and ran out of the room, slamming the door behind me! That was one of the most awkward moments of my life, but I needed my asthma inhaler, it was essential to calming down the wheezing in my throat! It was worth it in the end; the simple puffer calmed down my breathing and within minutes I felt relief. It was awkward for the rest of the season with my housemate, but after that moment she spent more time at Shane's to enjoy his passionate embrace without disturbance!

I loved the perks of working at Buller Sports, especially the free ski and snowboard lessons. I tried snowboarding and I found it so difficult. I spent most of the time with my butt in the snow. But I was grateful that I had the opportunity to try a sport that I had never embarked on before.

Being a skier suited me better, I loved the freedom of casting down the mountains and moving my feet back and forth through the snow. My first lesson was difficult, but I soon broke past the beginner stage and started to enjoy ski runs around Mt Buller.

It was amazing. I ended up attending intermediate ski classes, which were three hours long. I learnt to parallel ski. This is when the skis stay parallel to each other all the time, no matter what you are doing. I was used to the beginner snow-plough technique, which is otherwise known as the pizza. I felt comfortable using the pizza method, as I could stop at any time and I could control my speed and turn.

When I parallel skied, I had to let go of fear and just go down the mountain. It is amazing, some of the children that attended these classes held no fear. They just zoomed down the mountain. I told myself to be like these children. Just don't let fear get to you. Once you do, you lose momentum and suddenly, you're crashing into the snow. There was this one moment when I stacked down the Burnt Hut run; I was doing fine then I let fear take over.

Suddenly, I fell to the side and my skis came flying off. I wasn't injured badly, and a few people rushed over to help me get up again. I was scared of the speed when I should have really embraced it and just have gone with the flow. When you get older, you become more aware of how you can injure yourself. When you are a child, you don't care. You don't think about the consequences, you just go with the flow. There is no fear.

One of my favourite times were my days off. I got to take the free staff shuttle bus to Mansfield, otherwise known as Mansvegas, where I did grocery shopping. It was a lot cheaper than buying in Mt Buller, where the prices were very expensive for everyday food items. I enjoyed simple days where I would enjoy the sun or just have a coffee with friends. I love small towns, they are so quaint and have so much character.

I was a lot better working in a retail store, and my personality got to shine in a people-oriented role. The other perks of working at Buller Sports was that we got free equipment hire. By the end of the season, I was confident to ski down one of the hardest tracks with the support of my friend.

Some of my favourite moments were simply nights out, where we would create drunken snow angels and just giggle in the cold. We had many fun nights out, where we would dress up and join theme parties. It was funny, it was so cold outside but underneath the warm jackets not much was on! Especially during 'Sexy Schoolgirls' night. One of my housemates stuffed mountain hiking socks down her bra. She asked me if her boobs were big enough. I replied, 'Yeah, and if your feet get wet, you have a spare set of socks!'

If you ever work a ski season, most of your money goes on rent, food and alcohol! The majority of the people working at Mt Buller would follow the snow, working in both Australia and Canada. Working in the snow was a unique way of life and I can see how people would follow the snow all year around, especially if you love skiing!

Chapter 10
Dreamworld Life

Lesson: Have fun at staff parties. But try not to drink alcohol too much. You need to look after yourself too.

For those who need a heads up, there is a mention in this chapter of a non-consensual experience I had on a night out.

After working the ski season, I decided to follow the sun and applied to work at Dreamworld on the Gold Coast. I was back to pursuing my goal of working at every theme park around the world.

I ended up getting an interview, and flew up to attend the group interview with Beenleigh Training Centre. I was nervous, but confident that with my experience, I would get the ride operator position.

After the interview, I received a phone call. My application was successful! I soon started planning my move to the sunny Gold Coast.

I initially stayed at a backpackers' accommodation in Surfers Paradise, while trying to find long-term accommodation during the season. It was great to be surrounded by people from all over the world. However, I soon learnt my lesson not to be too trusting. While I was in the pool, my room was robbed. They took my wallet and my friend's phone.

This robbery threw a spanner in the works. I could not go to work as I had no money for the bus. So, I had to take the day off to prove my identity to the bank and cancel all debit and credit cards.

Since then, I have carried a lock with me while travelling, you just never know who you're sharing a room with!

That first season at Dreamworld was so much fun, I loved going to work every day. It was amazing to be part of such a huge theme park team.

What I loved most about Dreamworld was the people, everyone was so friendly and made it a pleasure to go to work every day.

As my shifts started early, I had to catch the bus, then the train to Coomera Station, then walk my way towards Dreamworld. It wasn't a bad walk, but it was a bit horrible as there was very little in the way of footpaths. Pretty much, Dreamworld felt like it was in the middle of nowhere! Nearly every day during the peak season, I would find myself tripping over a stick or a random stone! Walking wasn't for the fainthearted, but I eventually made it to the entrance of Dreamworld. After work, I could catch the direct bus, which would take me to Helensvale Station, which was a lot less painful than the big walk!

I loved orientation, especially being able to pat a tiger cub. It was so amazing to be so close to such a beautiful creature that would bring joy to hundreds of people every day.

My favourite ride to help operate was the Wipeout, it was so cool. I loved using our special hand signals, checking seat belts and making sure passengers were safe. I also had a giggle watching the faces of the customers, the pure exhilaration or fright taking over from their cool exteriors as they entered the Wipeout.

At the time, the girl band, The Veronicas, were visiting Dreamworld at their peak of fame. Band members, Lisa and Jess, decided that they would go on the Wipeout. It was amazing to see how two people could inspire teenagers to scream very loud.

When Jess and Lisa walked into the ride, I was surprised at how small they were. I noticed it again when I had to ensure their restraints were locked in securely.

My supervisor also came around to double-check that everything was running smoothly. When I watched Jess and Lisa go upside down on the Wipeout, it was funny to see their normally cool demeanours change to huge smiles and screams of fright. It really made me think that you could be the most famous person in the world, but you're just human like everyone else. You can scream and take humour in the little things in life.

I loved the wardrobe department. It was amazing how many uniforms, in so many colours, were used across the theme park. Every morning you would wait to receive a freshly laundered uniform and then get ready for the day. It was a very organised process, and I have great admiration for the wardrobe department, who managed to pump out the uniforms for hundreds of staff during a day.

What Dreamworld is known for is the staff parties, they were truly amazing. Every year we had a theme for the Christmas Parties, and it was so much fun to go on rides, even though I don't recommend going on rides after a few drinks. There was one stage where I thought it was a great idea to go on the Wipeout after a few drinks because all my friends were doing it! When I was up in the air, vomit started to creep up my throat. I was so anxious about the ride closing because of my vomit that I managed to push down the bile rising up from my throat. I don't recommend doing that! It was like a slow, ripe burn churning down my neck!

I don't recommend getting too drunk at staff parties, especially in a work environment that is seasonal. Sure, you make friendships, but you're only briefly in their life. You're friends for one season, and when the holiday period is over, you may never see that person again. I remember one time I had too many drinks and one of the people we were hanging out with tried to take advantage of me. In my drunken state, I was very vulnerable. My friends at the time thought I was enjoying his company, but it was the complete opposite. At the end of the night, we all got a lift to the train station. I was left alone with him when the others departed on the train to Brisbane. I remember feeling very frightened. He kept pulling me back and trying to kiss me.

I still had some coherence, and managed to break his embrace and pull the doors open to the safety of the train. The bright lights and safety of the train was welcoming. I finally escaped his unwelcome touch and was on the way home to recover from the night. From that moment I realised, if I was with friends on a night out, how important it was to check in and make sure that they are ok. They may look ok on the outside, but that honestly could look deceiving. Alcohol does so many bad things to your judgement and you could be left in a harmful situation that you are incapable of escaping. Luckily, I never saw that person again and I honestly believe I had an angel on my shoulder helping me out.

What I thought would be just one season at Dreamworld turned into four! Despite that experience, I loved working at the theme park and didn't let it affect my enjoyment of the job.

I ended up staying and studying on the Gold Coast for five years!

Chapter 11
Study

**Lesson: Study a craft that you love.
Embrace learning it can be enjoyable.**

I studied tourism at Gold Coast Institute of TAFE and then, using my grades, went on to study a Bachelor of Arts majoring in Journalism, Public Relations and Marketing at Griffith University.

I absolutely loved studying. If I could be a University student the rest of my life, I would do that in a heartbeat. However, it does depend on what I'm studying. It has to be a topic that I love.

My time at Griffith University was an opportunity to indulge my love of writing. As a child, I had many pen pals from around the world and I loved learning about different cultures through the simple act of letter writing. I am still in contact with my pen pals all these years later, through Facebook. It's funny, I feel like through writing we grew up together, in a way, as we shared our lives on a monthly basis.

There is something special about receiving a handwritten letter in the mail. There is a certain effort placed into those simple strokes of the hand, and in a way, a letter shows a person's spirit. Loud cursive could mean maybe you're a bit excited to be writing. Tight cursive means maybe you're a perfectionist and like putting the little details in a script. I like to imagine the person behind the letter, especially since we have never met in person. I like to let my imagination take over and my creative spirit soar.

I loved writing about people and the way they change the world in their own little way. I remember writing a series of interviews on performers on the Gold Coast, and I stumbled across retirees Bram and Marina Nicolson, who, as *Double the Fun*, sang at nursing homes and respite centres. I loved their enthusiasm to inject some joy into the lives of residents. Years later, when I did my placement at a nursing home, I would realise what an incredible role Bram and Marina played in making the life of a resident better. Little did I know that this first interview would be one of many that I would conduct with seniors over the years. Another little seed starting to sprout into a big dream.

Chapter 12
Casual Work on the G.C.

Lesson: Ask questions. Be curious. Get to know people you may find out something interesting.

While on the Gold Coast, I ended up working at many major events, through All Crowd Catering, and Spotless. Every weekend, I would be working either a game of rugby at Suncorp Stadium, or football at Carrara Stadium, now called Metricon Stadium. I didn't really understand rugby, but I loved how excited the fans became when they saw their team score a touchdown. I used to work in the corporate area as a food runner, it was hard work delivering food and drink to guests. But I loved getting to know the other staff from around the world. There were a lot of people from Brazil and Colombia, and I loved getting to know their culture and way of life. I would love to go to Brazil and Colombia one day, they are such wonderful people, full of colour and life!

Working in the corporate areas was another world, I got to see celebrities such as Shane Webcke, who is a former professional rugby player for the Brisbane Broncos. Nearly every weekend, Shane was there in his corporate box, while I was in the corridors delivering food and beverages. My friends who grew up in Queensland were envious, I was working in amongst rugby royalty and I still had no idea how the game was run. Being amongst these rugby greats was wasted on a girl from Victoria!

I remember one time my friend said she served Kevin Rudd, the Former Prime Minister of Australia. Kevin was in one of her corporate suites, and she was so nervous. She asked Kevin if he would like a chocolate, he replied jovially that he should be watching his weight.

This moment really brought Kevin down to our level, and made me realise that even though he held a really important role, he was just human, like us.

My favourite event to work was the Gold Coast Show, where I would be either the cashier in the food or coffee van. I loved the ding of the cash register and the fast pace of the job. I enjoyed yelling out orders and prepping containers for food. I didn't really have to think that much, I would just go on autopilot! Sometimes we would have massive queue lines, especially in the mornings. People wanted their coffee and they wanted it fast! I never wanted to be a barista; the job looked too stressful. You would have to remember all the little details such as if they needed soy milk or regular milk, or how to create a coffee drink like Affogato in minutes. I was always grateful for my breaks, where I would enjoy a free meal from the company and just relax and enjoy a half hour of peace. When you work with hordes of people, those minutes away are really important so you can calm down. After working at a fast rate, I found I needed to just slow down and to enjoy just being in the moment.

After the shift I would potter around the showground, playing with the animals, watching shows and buying showbags. That was my special treat for such a long day.

Working at the Big Day Out made my housemates very jealous. One of my housemates very cheekily applied for a job at the catering company, just so he could get in for free. His plan, once he was hired, was to ditch work and enjoy the Big Day Out. He asked me to be one of his references. While I admired his ambition to enjoy a concert for free, I declined. Even though this was just a casual role, my word of mouth meant so much. I needed this job to help me survive through university.

People paid a lot of money to watch these bands, and I got to hear them for free while I worked. There were some headlining acts which included Metallica and The Black Eyed Peas, but I didn't really get to enjoy them, I was too busy serving the huge queue lines of customers wanting their burgers!

I did get to enjoy some of the concert after my shift, but to be honest, I had my joy watching people in their crazy outfits. I love to people-watch, and some of their outfits were out-there. There was your mainstream fashion, from flowy white dresses with flowers in your hair to bare midriffs and short shorts. Then the crazy outfits: tie-dye shirts, large afros and ripped clothing! It was amazing the large spectrum of outfits which captivated my attention!

I also did have random chats with people in the huge line for the bathrooms. I remember talking to this lady who was bragging that at the age of 28, she was a doctor. After a few drinks, she was happily slurring about operations and body parts. In amongst body part talks, she announced proudly that she had brought her own toilet paper!

While I was studying, I landed a market research job in a call centre. The role was pretty convenient as the office was located a short distance from my home, which meant I could walk to work. All I had to do was call former students from a local university and ask them questions about their career choices, and if what they studied at university had prepared them well for the role they had now.

Sometimes it was difficult, as people are always suspicious of phone interviews, but once you tell them the survey was on the behalf of the university, this built a certain level of trust. I remember one time I had to ask a doctor these survey questions, and he said, 'If you can do the survey fast, then yes.' I had to squeeze a 10-minute survey into 5 minutes. It was literally a blur of yes and no answers. There was one stage I was struggling to breathe, as I was saying the questions so fast. At the end of the interview, the doctor said, 'Are you ok?' I replied, 'Yes.' Then he said he thought I was going to have a heart attack, I was talking so fast. Well, he asked for a fast survey, and I delivered beyond expectation! I did need a good puff of my asthma pump afterwards, as I was short of breath.

One time, while the main boss was away, one of my co-workers was doing a usual survey, and at first it started as a mainstream job. Then this 10-minute survey ended in a 30-minute chat. She was talking about her fitness routine and how she likes to keep fit. She ended up writing down his number and they met up in real life at the local pub. I was pretty amazed, from one simple conversation she had managed to organise a first date! It wasn't true love when they met up in person. She said he was too young and wasn't as mature as she wanted. But at least she took a cheeky chance at love, not many romance stories do bloom from a phone call, that's for sure! I was surprised she wasn't fired after that phone call, as I'm sure she would have broken a lot of rules to make that date happen.

After five years of living on the Gold Coast, I decided to move back to Melbourne to find a job that suited my University degree. I had tried so hard to find a communications position on the Gold Coast, but often I would bump into fellow graduates. I hated that those that had studied alongside me were now considered my competition. Getting a job you love is tough, because everyone else wants the same job!

Maybe it was a good thing that I was unsuccessful in gaining a position. I believe the universe has a funny way of putting you on the right path!

Chapter 13
Back Home to Melbourne

Lesson: Sometimes rejection hurts. Don't take it to heart. One day you will find a dream job or create your own!

When I arrived back home in Melbourne, it was so nice to be surrounded by family and my beloved dog, Bunny. At first, I didn't worry about getting a job. But then what happened on the Gold Coast occurred in Melbourne! No matter how hard I tried to find a proper full-time job, I would either get a rejection email or an interview where I would be rejected!

Getting rejected so much really hurt my confidence. I became quite depressed, and the only way out was to find a casual job that I would thrive doing well.

While applying for work, I stumbled across a job serving soft drinks and water at the St Kilda Festival, which is an event held every year in February. It attracts more than 300,000 people, making it one of the largest outdoor celebrations in Australia.

I thought the St Kilda Festival would be good fun, and I could listen to some great bands while working. I decided to apply and was offered the job within one week! It was a pretty fast process, all I had to do was attend an orientation and *bingo*, I started on Saturday.

My uniform was pretty simple, all I needed was a black top and pants, and I was ready to go. When I arrived in St Kilda, it wasn't so busy. It was at 9 am and I was due to work at 10 am. I could see the morning joggers and people enjoying breakfast along Acland Street. The familiar ding of the trams running along the main road brought back memories of working at Luna Park, which felt like a second home to me.

I was shown the catering van where I would be working. It was a pretty small space, but I was used to working in compact places, thanks to my work for the catering company on the Gold Coast. At least I wasn't working with alcohol, which made the job easier. Dealing with drunk patrons can be tough, especially if you have to refuse service to customers if they have consumed too much alcohol.

Soon it started to get busy and people started piling in. I was lucky, I was close to the stage in the O'Donnell Gardens, where I got to see some great local musicians singing some fun tunes, and a DJ spinning some great tracks to whittle the night away.

I was lucky to be matched up with a great co-worker who was good at math, we were pumping out the drinks fast. Sometimes it was hard to calculate in my head how much the change was. But at least the math was easy, the soft drinks were $5.00, which was so expensive, but people were willing to pay. Most could not be bothered to go to the supermarket and would prefer to just grab a drink out of convenience and enjoy a free band.

After working for the St Kilda Festival, I decided to embark on the industries that I thrived in, and once again I was on the hunt for customer service jobs. I was very lucky to land jobs both at the Melbourne Cricket Club and Marvel Stadium. I was so grateful to be employed again and my confidence slowly started to return.

Chapter 14

Events Industry

Lesson: Everyone is human. No matter how big or small their status in the world. As my mum says Everyone poops.

I was in my element in the events industry. Both roles at Marvel Stadium and Melbourne Cricket Club involved working with patrons from all around the world. All I had to do was provide information on the venue, and show patrons to their seats. Through these roles, I got to see wicked concerts like Adele and Bon Jovi, while getting paid. My favourite concert was Adele, who played at what was known as Etihad Stadium at the time. She was amazing.

I was pretty close to the stage and once I ushered everyone to their seats, I got to relax and enjoy the concert. She has such a great sense of humour, and I loved her banter in between songs.

Adele totally blew me away with her humble account of her life to where she was now. Adele painted a colourful character, and it was like a mini comedy show. I could not stop smiling. She chatted about burping and what it was like at the Oscars, with her 'tits overflowing with milk,' after having a child. She revealed that while her life looks glamourous, she was really wearing a diamond encrusted dress, drawing in sweat and bugs!

I liked how she shared her personal photos from when she was growing up. As a child, she had a big smile on her face, and loved East 17. I, too, had a poster of the East 17 gang on my wall! It was nice reminiscing about the past and fond memories. I also loved the personal touch of Adele's handwritten notes that were plastered all over the stadium, that was truly lovely. Such a wonderful concert that shows you can be humble and famous.

I remember when Justin Bieber played at Etihad Stadium, he totally took me by surprise. To be honest, I was not a huge fan of his. He seemed to have a huge attitude when captured by the media. All his tattoos and bad attitude may have been a big hit with teenagers, but it would take a lot to change my viewpoint of him.

While waiting for briefing to start, we were sitting in the seats overlooking the stadium. It was the calm before hundreds of teenagers would scream their way into Etihad Stadium. Then all of sudden, this sense of calm was broken with the tapping of a soccer ball rolling around the ground. I looked up from my briefing notes and spotted this bleached haired kid running around kicking a ball. At first, I thought it was a dancer, fitting in some exercise. Then I looked closer. It was Justin Bieber. He seemed so young and innocent, kicking around a ball. He was not with an entourage of people. He was just himself, deep in his thoughts, kicking a ball. Sometimes you build up so much hype around a celebrity that you forget they are just human. As my mum says, everyone has to poop, no matter what status you are in life.

In a few hours, Justin would be on stage singing his songs to thousands of screaming fans. But I will always remember him as that bleached haired kid, kicking around the ball.

I loved working at the MCG, and I felt privileged to be part of the wonderful atmosphere of major events, such as the Grand Final. There is nothing better than two teams battling hard to win the much sought after AFL Premiership Cup.

The best AFL Grand Final I worked at was in 2018, when the two teams were Collingwood and West Coast. It was amazing to be a part of the atmosphere, where every part of the MCG felt like passion for Collingwood was oozing out of every seat. I loved how some people dressed up to support their team, especially Collingwood fans. Some fans looked like Vikings ready to battle, with their faces painted black and white. The fans had their Collingwood flags waving in the air, goading their arch nemesis, the West Coast Eagles. Nearly every seat was dominated by black and white, with a little bit of blue and yellow representing the West Coast Eagles, ready to snatch the AFL Premiership Cup. The MCG was a full house, with 100,022 spectators from all around Australia ready to see their team rumble for the Premiership Cup.

When the siren signalled the match was ready to go, for literally every minute, I was on the edge of my seat to see who would be the winner. It was a head-to-head match where either team could have won. I was hypnotized by the athletic grace each player had. The ball bounced from one end to the other, with goals hard to make on either side. Each side had their battle faces, eager to bring home the Premiership Cup. Towards the end, it looked like Collingwood was going for the win. Then West Coast suddenly got a burst of energy and they swooped in, kicking goals, beating Collingwood by five points.

The Collingwood fans were devastated, some even crying and banging the side of their chair. The moment of victory was so close, yet so far. I have never seen fans get so emotional before. Some fans drank so much they ended up being kicked out of the MCG. It was like their team had died, and the fans were wallowing deep in grief. Watching Collingwood President Eddie McGuire on the big screen seemed cruel. He had his eyes closed and you could see tears drip down his face. This was a moment in history that would spark sadness in any Collingwood die-hard fan. I felt sorry for those who were so eager to see their home team win. But I was happy for West Coast, they worked so hard and now they could take home the Premiership Cup. There will always be another grand final, where Collingwood may have the opportunity to play once again.

What I also love about the grand final is the free concert at the end. I always end up going with my workmates, it is such a fun way to celebrate the end of the football season. One of my favourite concerts was way back in 2014, when Ed Sheeran was the supporting act for Tom Jones. Back then, Ed Sheeran was not that well known. I absolutely loved the ginger-haired English bloke. Ed had us all up and dancing to his songs. His songs held such joy and the soulful tunes would get everyone's head bopping. I felt like we were witness to a rising star. And in a few years, Ed Sheeran would hold his own concerts in Australia where he would be the lead singer.

Just recently, in March 2020, I had worked the final of the ICC Women's T20 World Cup. It was such a massive turnout, with 80,000 fans eager to celebrate International Woman's Day with a fun day at the cricket.

As icing on the cake, international pop star Katy Perry was the headlining entertainment. It was wonderful to see fans supporting women in sport and so many people passionate about celebrating the power of being female. I didn't see much of the cricket, as I was located on the outside of the MCG, assisting customers who had won the ballot to see Katy Perry on the arena after the match. There was so many people excited that they could see their idol from the green grass of the famous MCG, with some flying interstate so they could be in Melbourne just for Katy Perry! There were so many fans begging to have extra wristbands so their friends could join them at the concert. In a way, I felt sad that they could not join their friends, but I had to be tough. Many people applied to win tickets to the arena, and it would have been unfair if I gave these much sought after wristbands to those that did not take part in the ballot.

Towards the end of the cricket match, I had to walk down a crowded aisle bay to assist customers with any questions about the Katy Perry concert at 10 pm. It was pretty scary walking down the crowded bay, it was very narrow and many people were pushing their way down to get a good view of the awards ceremony, where the women's Australian cricket team won the match against India.

While walking down the stairs of the aisle, I could smell a strong smell of sweat, which made me want to escape into a quiet place. All the smells and noise can become quite overwhelming after a while. After the awards ceremony, I had to push through fans to the very front, where the door to the green grass of the MCG was located. After reaching the door, I was told I had to wait until I was given the signal to open the door to reach the safety of the green grass.

After what felt like hours, I was finally let out onto the grass. For one hour, I was pressed against the front of the bay, dealing with customers anxious about running onto the ground. I had fans speculate that they would get crushed, and others complain about the long waiting time. No matter what I said to calm down their nerves, nothing worked. I was stuck waiting against the door, looking forward to escaping into my own space.

When I was allowed onto the ground, it was like a sweet relief. I could laugh with the security guards and chat to the Indian cheer squad who were amused about all the fuss over Katy Perry. When I asked one of the Indian fans if he was going to stay and watch the concert, he replied, 'No, I'm hungry, my favourite part of the night will be when there is room for us to walk up the aisles.' He made me laugh so hard. While I was surrounded by Katy Perry fans, this Indian man just cared about food.

Finally, the clock ticked 10 pm. It was time to let the fans of Katy Perry onto the ground. I was grateful I had security guards assisting me. There was so many fans excited about seeing Katy Perry that they tried to push their way down the aisle. It was scary to see so many people unconcerned about safety that they didn't care if they were to push someone over.

We had to let customers go onto the ground one by one. Only opening the door to let one customer through. We asked the customers to put their hands with the wristband in the air so we could see if they had appropriate wristbands. Some fans tried to get into the ground by placing the green confetti, that had been blasted out during the awards ceremony, onto their wrists. When we asked why they had placed the green confetti on their wrists, they replied, 'Oh, we thought it was for anybody who had a green tag.' We also had a lady who wanted to pick a fight with the security guard as she didn't want to show her wristband. In the end, she showed us the appropriate wristband. But she had quite a few ticked off customers behind her who were annoyed they had to wait behind her. She wanted to create a fight out of simply showing her wristband.

After letting the fans onto the ground, it was time to relax and enjoy the concert. I was at the southern end of the MCG, which was pretty far from where the main concert was being held. I was content to watch the TV showing Katy Perry dancing and singing. I loved how she manages to make a show entertaining by not only her voice, but her fun costumes. Her outfits were bright pink, and she was surrounded by dancers dressed as cricket bats with eyes and bright pink lips! Katy did pretty well, as she was pregnant at the time.

The concert went until 11.30 pm, but I had escaped at 11 pm. I wanted to catch the train before the mass of fans reached Richmond Station. Sometimes that can be the worst part of the night, waiting to get through the ticket barriers into the station where so many people are hustling to get the train home!

One of the most important lessons I had learnt from working at the MCG came from one of my colleagues, who worked as a cleaner. Despite her age, she could tackle this physical job so well, but at times I could see a glimmer of tiredness etched around her eyes. Walking up and down stairs and all over the stadium can take it out of anyone, but she just keeps going. She always had a big smile on her face and said hello to me. Patrons love her. She had that certain personality that you just can't miss. She told me with a big sigh that sometimes when you're a cleaner, people don't look at you. They don't see you. You're treated like crap. I replied that it's a shame, we are all human, regardless of what position we are in, regardless of what pay we receive. Sometimes the most amazing people are those who thrive in the background. And I will always have the highest respect for her. She is a battler and, in this world, that can be one of the best traits you can have. Work with what you have. Not who people believe you to be.

Chapter 15

Volunteering at Business Chicks

Lesson: Volunteer at major events. You get to make new friends and enjoy an event in exchange for your labour. Also, lots of free stuff!

All throughout my life, I've always loved volunteering for major events that otherwise would be too expensive to attend as a delegate.

I love being behind the scenes of a major event and seeing the main organisers lead their volunteers and staff to cater for the little things that matter.

I've been volunteering for Business Chicks since 2014, and my first crewing experience was for Julia Gillard, who was speaking at the Crown Casino in Melbourne. She was promoting her book, *My Story*, and was sharing her views on what it was like to be the first female prime minister of Australia in 2010.

I have been a big fan of Julia Gillard, and I was looking forward to seeing her talk live and in person. Tickets to see Julia were expensive, from memory I think it was $190, and the only way I could afford to see her was to volunteer my time.

The only issue with volunteering for Business Chicks is that their breakfast events start bright and early! Meaning I would often have to stay at the local YHA, which is a backpackers' accommodation located a short walk from the Crown Casino, in order to make the early 5.30 am starts.

Volunteering for a major event starts the day prior, everyone who volunteers is required to assist with venue set-up. During my first day, when I walked into the Crown Casino Garden Room, I was amazed to see such camaraderie from the beginning. I thought mainly event students were going to be the major volunteers, but there was a range of age groups, young and old. Some were students, others just wanted to be a part of something exciting. Everyone was crowded along three main tables with products donated by sponsors ready to be placed in goodie bags. When I joined the other volunteers, we created a production line and it was like a fine-tuned team. Soon we had filled over 100 pink Business Chicks bags full of products, ranging from T2 Tea, to candles. It was pretty hard work and my back ached at the end; we really did work hard to see Julia Gillard, that's for sure!

When you attend an event as a delegate, the last thing you think about is what order the sponsors' brochures are in, or that flyer on the top of your napkin. I found out that it's these little details that make an event successful. Even though Business Chicks received these products for free, businesses pay big bucks to have their products in front of their ideal audiences. All the people attending the Julia Gillard event were exposed to these products, and may use these products long-term, which was an investment to those promoting their goods and services. We had to ensure that businesses that paid the most had top priority for their brochures and products. I never really thought about this, but when putting out the products on the tables and in the goodie bags, we had to make sure they were placed in a certain order, and that products were well presented on the table. Every detail mattered, and the Business Chicks team ensured that everything was as per the brief of every sponsor that took part in the day. It seemed like a lot of work to keep advertisers happy, but it was worth it in the end. Their sponsorship provided jobs and assisted in making the event successful.

After setting up tables, we had a small break to enjoy a few snacks and have a chat about the reasons we were volunteering our time. Most of the students talked about how they wanted to get event set-up experience. But I didn't really have much of an agenda about gaining experience. When I got asked that question, I felt weird not being an event student and not really caring about the experience. All I wanted was to see one of my idols, and the best way to do so was to volunteer my time. I also enjoy working with students, and imparting some of my knowledge with them.

We were then assigned roles and I put my hand up to be part of the registration team. This involved setting up the name badges and greeting guests as they arrived. I would then issue guests with a name tag if they were in my section. It seemed like a pretty cruisy gig. The other roles included assisting guests with table directions, holding a bowl to collect business cards, customer ticketing issues, book sales and general ushering assistance.

After three hours, I was pretty tuckered out and eager to grab some dinner at the food court. I scored some cheap Chinese food and then after, made my way to my hostel room for the night.

I was so lucky to have roommates at the YHA who did not mind that I would be up at 4.30 am to get ready for the Business Chicks function. I was lucky that the event finished at 9.30 am so I could still store my bags in the room without having to pay for a locker to store all my gear, as check out was at 10 am. At 4.30 am, my alarm went off. I had my headphones on so I could hear the alarm. It wasn't the most rested sleep as I was constantly checking my phone to see if it was 4.30 am. I turned on my torch and collected my clothes, slowly shuffling into the bathroom to have a quick shower.

I had managed to get myself ready by 5.20 am, and started to walk towards the Crown Casino. It was so weird being up so early in the city, it felt like it was nighttime, as it was still dark. The city looks so beautiful, and was haunting as it was so quiet. I loved the chirp of the early morning birds and the soft lights on the Yarra River. There were a few people jogging along the Yarra, and it was nice to see them getting a head start on their day. However, I was craving a coffee, I wasn't an early morning person!

I eventually made it to the Crown Casino and was amazed to see how beautiful the room was. The colour pink was in abundance with the Business Chicks banners on proud display. I loved the little details, such as in the bathrooms, there were little signs with inspirational quotes, and free period pads for those that needed it. Every small detail counted, even to the Business

Chicks goodie bags, plastered with questions such as, *What's your super power?*

Julie Gillard popped out to say a quick hello and then was quickly ushered into the green room. It was nice of her to make an effort to say hi.

I was surprised at how many people made it to an early breakfast event. It was great these events can be squeezed in before a day of work, and that even before 9 am you can be inspired by someone amazing.

Even though a lot of people collected their name badges, I was sad that still there were many people that did not attend. Their companies paid for them to come and enjoy Julia Gillard, but because of the early morning, most would have preferred their bed! I thought it was such a shame, as these tickets are expensive, and maybe a university student would have loved to go on a waiting list to take their spot. Julia had so much knowledge to share to those even on a tight budget!

I love that Business Chicks do things a little bit differently. Most people collect their badges by surname, but Business Chicks puts the first name first. It seems more personal, and a lot of people preferred being referred to by their first name.

After the bulk of people received their name badges, we were ushered to the back of the room to listen to Julia Gillard. It was such a popular event that it looked like all the tables were full of eager women, enjoying breakfast, waiting to be motived and inspired by Julia.

Soon it came time for Julia to come on stage where she was greeted by journalist Sandra Sully, who proceeded to interview Julia about her time in parliament. Julia seemed really engaging and humble. She seemed to focus on her achievements and challenges and how she faced them.

I loved how Julia talked about her unforgettable misogyny speech held during parliament. She spoke passionately about how women should support women, and made me proud to be amongst many women in the room who had their own businesses or held a critical role in their own workplace.

It is funny, Julia had achieved so much as Prime Minister. But when she had to step down from that role, her first obstacle was learning how to drive again. She could not remember how to drive. I had a little giggle when she said she often finds herself the victim of finger pointing and gesturing at the lights, not because of who she is, but because she has been driving at 22 kilometres an hour.

Volunteering at the Julia Gillard event was just one of the many events that I have enjoyed with Business Chicks. Business Chicks treat their volunteers well. In exchange for our time, we receive a goodie bag full of products, and that is pretty exciting. I have tried so many fun products that I otherwise could never afford or splurge on, and for that I am also grateful! I would recommend volunteering for Business Chicks, as it provides an insider perspective on how a successful event is run, and it is also fun.

Chapter 16
The Seeds of a Business Idea

**Lesson: If you have an idea. Just give it a go.
You will lose nothing but gain so much experience.**

I had heard about the New Enterprise Initiative Scheme, which is a program devised to assist people with the creation of a business. I was really interested in taking part of the program. I hated applying for jobs and always getting rejected. I thought if I created my own business and made a profit, I could become my own boss and take back the power of always having my working fate in another person's hands.

But what would I sell? A few months prior, I had created a CD full of photos, which I had timed to music for my Uncle Peter. I had scanned the photos and touched them up in Photoshop to take away the damage done over time.

I thought, I could sell that! I went to an information session and applied for the program. I was lucky enough to get into the NEIS program and set about creating a business plan for Golden Days Images, focused on creating products that preserved photos in a fun, creative way.

What I thought would be a great way to gain some traction for the business was to create an exhibition at the local Frankston venue, B'Artiste. I could generate some interest by interviewing Frankston seniors and gathering their stories to be cherished in the local community. I had no idea how to create an exhibition, but I didn't let that stop me. I figured, *I'll work it out as I go.*

I realised that the only seniors in my life were my parents. My Grandmother had passed away many years ago, and I rarely had contact with the older generations.

I decided to look through the local papers and find out what community groups were attractive to seniors. The first community group was Frankston National Seniors, which is held every last Wednesday of the month.

I didn't know who to contact ahead of time, so I decided to just rock up and let fate decide how the group will react to my appearance.

What I had assumed would be a small gathering turned out to be a huge group. I literally nearly ran away when I peeked into the church hall. I didn't realise that I would be asking to speak in front of a huge audience.

But then I realised the worst that could happen was that I would get turned away because I am not a senior.

I ran into the toilet, calmed down my nerves, and crept into the church hall.

Suddenly I was stopped by a senior who asked, with a huge look of confusion, 'Are you here to join us?'

I sheepishly answered, 'Ah yes, I'm organising an exhibition showcasing local seniors in Frankston, and was wondering if I could speak to your group?'

She told me to speak to their marketing manager, and he said, 'Yes, you can speak during the tea break. Take a seat.'

The meeting soon started, and what I assumed would be oldies sipping tea and eating scones, turned out to be a fun meeting.

They had their morning melodies, where everyone sang and played random instruments. It was really a nice start to the day.

Soon it was time to speak and I was handed a microphone. I said, 'I can speak loud enough, do I really need this microphone?'

At first, they let me speak without the microphone, then I realised why they were keen for me to use the microphone

Suddenly there was a loud banging from the back of the church hall. I looked up and saw three men banging on the tables, yelling, 'Speak louder!'

I was in shock. I thought seniors were meant to be sweet, not rowdy! I felt like they were the naughty kids in a classroom, breaking the stereotype I had envisioned of seniors sitting together, chatting over tea and scones!

I managed to talk about how I was organising an exhibition and needed to interview and photograph seniors. By the end of the meeting, I had three people interested in participating, and they had friends from the local retirement village who wanted to get involved.

I was happy that I broke through my nerves and managed to speak to a church full of seniors. I didn't look like I was nervous, but this was the start of my faking-it-until-I-got-the-trust-of-the-seniors stage.

Sometimes it can be hard to get trust from a senior, you have to be consistent and open to listening. You can't just rock up to a meeting without them expecting you! From then, I made sure if I would turn up, that I asked for permission to attend the next meeting to gather a few more people for the exhibition.

Chapter 17
The Beginning of Celebrate Living History

**Lesson: Be open to new opportunities.
Talk to people and discover their stories.**

Little did I know, I would go on to create an organisation called Celebrate Living History, focused on connecting seniors with young journalism students. This exhibition provided the foundation for Celebrate Living History to grow.

I continued to speak at many other community groups on the Mornington Peninsula and surrounding areas.

Some of my favourites included the Frankston Ladies Probus, where I joined everyone with a cup of tea. Everyone had their own teacup and told the story behind the cup. One of the ladies had a really old cup that featured the Queen when she was young. Her eyes sparkled as she spoke fondly of the excitement when the Queen took over the throne.

Another highlight was the Mentone Probus. I was next in line to speak after a guy from the Lost Dogs' Home. A senior was having a gentle snooze in the back. Suddenly the Lost Dogs' Home speaker started blowing on his whistle around his neck. The old bloke woke up very startled, and it was hilarious seeing his face! The Lost Dogs' Home speaker said he had done a lot of talks at community groups and learnt that he needed a whistle around his neck, ready to wake people up. He was definitely prepared for any senior sleeping encounter, that's for sure!

I never knew organising an exhibition could be so stressful. I thought all I had to do was find people to interview and take their photos. Maybe find some photos from their youth and Photoshop a little bit.

Some of my interviews took over three hours. At the time I didn't really have much experience keeping to a time limit. When a person talks about their life story, it can be hard to keep to one topic, when I can see all the little details come to life. I don't want to stop the momentum when that person ends up getting a twinkle in their eye and has a huge smile on their face, recalling fun times from their youth. In a way it felt like a verbal time travel to another world that I have never experienced before.

I loved that whole process. When a person starts telling their story with me, they don't know what to expect. They start off having a cup of tea, staring off into space. Then I literally see their minds tick and remember details. Their whole demeanour changes, they become more active with each word recalled.

At the time I didn't have a car, so I would be riding my bicycle to the difficult places that were hard to reach by public transport. I would put my tripod and video camera in my little basket and eventually get to the destination! I'm glad the interviews that I conducted were during a sunny time, when it was not raining. I was very lucky considering that I lived in Melbourne where the weather would change constantly, one minute its sunny the next pouring with rain. I'm sure I would not have looked very professional, soaking wet and dripping with rain. But I would have made do and tried my best, maybe even asking for a towel so I could become dryer and feel more like a human!

There was this one interview where at the end, I was asked where my motor vehicle was! He was staring right at my bicycle! I felt so ashamed at the time that I lied and said my car was parked around the corner. I said I got lost and walked the rest of the way. Looking back, I should not have been ashamed. I did so much with little money. I was using my initiative and resources to make an exhibition a reality.

I believe not having much experience as an artist came in handy.

I was oblivious to such things like professionally framing the photos of the seniors I had captured. I borrowed my mum's car, grabbed a trolley and walked right into Big W. I bought the most affordable frames in bulk and carted the frames out of the store. I think I looked a funny sight, the shop attendant looked so confused at the volume of frames I had purchased! I then went home and placed the photos carefully in the frames with Blu Tack! I did end up professionally framing some of the more iconic images, like my first photograph of Dorothy Dempster, who I had met while I was a volunteer at AMES – an organisation dedicated to assisting migrants learning English. She was one of the first people that I interviewed, and her image is one that makes me smile. I took her photograph at the AMES Christmas party, and she looked so joyful and full of life. It is amazing how one single moment of joy can be captured in a photograph.

Soon I had 60 images, all ready for an exhibition at B'Artiste. I was lucky at the time to have the support of my closest friends, with some even travelling from Melbourne to assist with set up. There is so much involved in organising an event, particularly with seniors involved. In my generation, I can just send an email or SMS, inviting everyone to the exhibition opening. However, with seniors, I had to take the time to write handwritten invitations and personally call those involved, so that they wouldn't forget the exhibition was on! Then, I also had to arrange catering. This was before people were pedantic about where the food comes from. I had asked my seniors to bring their own food to share from their generation, I thought it would be wonderful to taste food from another era. And it turned out to be such a great idea, there ended up being a magnificent spread of asparagus and butter sandwiches, scones and cream and a range of yummy baked goods, like pigs in a blanket and cake.

I was so grateful for my volunteer team that assisted in setting up. Creating an exhibition turned out to be more difficult than anticipated. I had so much pressure to have all the photographs ready before opening time. While it seemed like an easy task to do, we ran out of wire to hang the photographs. I decided to send my senior helpers, Bill and Alan, to Bunnings to buy the wire. They took such a long time that I got really worried that something had happened. Both Bill and Alan did not own mobile phones, so I decided to call Bunnings, and said I had lost my father Bill. The customer service attendant called out on the loudspeaker asking for Bill. Turned out, he wasn't at Bunnings. Where were they? I was under pressure from Carlos, the owner, to get all these photographs hung up in one hour. I wanted to break down and cry. Suddenly, both Bill and Alan arrived with the wire. Turned out, they had made a detour and were having a yarn at Bill's. I was so grateful they both turned up and were ok. We eventually got all the photographs hung up. And finally, we could relax. We celebrated by collapsing in Bayside food court and enjoying a meal.

We rushed back to my house. In all the drama of creating an exhibition, I didn't know what outfit to wear! I finally decided on an outfit, and we took some photos with my furry muse, Bunny the dog. My faithful companion and best buddy, Bunny was by my side from the very beginning of Celebrate Living History. She told me when it was time to take a break, and I enjoyed many walks and cuddles with her.

I was so grateful for that little break, where we could play with Bunny and have some time to realise the potential of what we had achieved.

Soon it was 4 pm, and I had a new volunteer, Nicole, who assisted in putting up signs and escorting seniors up the stairs. Reflecting back, it wasn't the best venue for seniors, but it was my first exhibition, so I didn't really have a choice. I had to take what I could. I was sure this exhibition would open doors, and maybe one day I will hold an exhibition at a better venue, more appropriate for older generations.

On top of the pressure of the exhibition, I was launching the Celebrate Living History magazine, full of stories I had collected over the year. I had borrowed my friend Gerry's projector, and she was surprised at how professional everything looked.

I was lucky to secure sponsorship for the magazine by knocking on graphic designers' doors in Frankston. I chatted to Tanya at Bat Design, and she was in line with my passion for documenting the stories of seniors in Frankston. Tanya spent most of her free time designing the Celebrate Living History magazine, and also created the Celebrate Living History logo. I am forever grateful for her assistance, and looking back, I was surprised that I did knock on doors. Even though it looks like I have a loud personality, I am quite shy when it comes to asking for help, and that's probably one of the main reasons why Celebrate Living History would struggle to make ends meet if I gave up all my casual jobs to just concentrate on the organisation. But to tell you the truth, I think I would get bored in one job, I love the variety. I don't think there has been any stage of my life that I didn't have many jobs.

What I loved the most about my first exhibition was the diverse range of people that attended. I didn't have just seniors attending, but their families and young grandchildren joining in on the fun. I also had members of the Frankston Business Network, which I had joined to network with, but I ended up really just having a few drinks and taking free stuff!

Running the exhibition inspired me to randomly fly up to the Gold Coast to visit Griffith University, where I had spent three years of my life studying. I wanted to see if I could work with journalism students, and have these students relate to seniors the way I did through simply documenting stories. I decided to see if my one of my favourite lecturers, Professor Stephen Stockwell, was in his office. I was a bit nervous as it had been a while since he last saw me, and I was thinking, *Will he remember who I was?* I ended up taking a long time procrastinating at my favourite coffee place on campus. But then I realised that I have to break through my own barriers and just ask, the worst that could happen would be that Stephen would say no.

I eventually made it to his office, and Stephen was on the floor surrounded by books. I knocked on the door and I think I gave him a fright! I said, 'Hi Stephen, I hope you remember me! I have an idea to create a journalism internship connecting seniors with young people! Am I able to work with some of your students?' Stephen, after the initial shock, said yes. This was the beginning of Celebrate Living History, an internship program focused on bringing generations together through documenting stories.

Chapter 18
Networking Drama

Lesson: Look beyond stereotypes. Sometimes what you see is not the whole picture

At the time I was told about the value of networking, so I joined many business groups. One function was held in the city, and I felt so special that I had spoiled myself to attend this function where I could meet one of my idols, Bec Derrington, who is the founder of SourceBottle – an online platform that connects journalists with everyday business owners. I had used SourceBottle to find people over 60 who are doing amazing things in business and in life. These people became part of the first issue of the Celebrate Living History magazine, where I asked them about the type of businesses they run and what inspired them. The function was two hours from home, but I was determined to make it. I embarked on two trains and walked the rest of the way, to end up at this funky little warehouse. I was amazed at how a space can be transformed into a piece of living art. The roof was covered in twinkling lights, and everything looked so coordinated. I saw a group of people and asked if I could sit on their table. We started the awkward conversation thing, and they ended up chatting to their mates for the rest of the night. I felt awkward, but at least I would enjoy a nice meal. I had been surprised, when we said yes to the invitation, that there was no option saying if you were allergic to something. I had assumed there was no nuts, surely. They would cater for those who had allergies, right?

I enjoyed listening to Bec and the other panel members chat about their businesses. In the end I did get a photo with Bec, even though I think she was embarrassed about having a fan girl! Looking back at the photo, my cheeks were flushed red. It was redder than usual, but I thought it was just due to the wine.

Soon the courses of food came out. Usually if I eat something that I'm allergic to, my tongue tingles as a warning sign. In this case, I had dulled my warning mechanism with wine. An hour after the meals, I started to get an itchy throat and decided to walk back to the station. I was ready to go home. As I approached the traffic lights, vomit started coming out of my throat. I was frightened. This was not normal, and I was worried if I fell down, I was in the middle of nowhere with no one to help. Or if someone saw me, they would just assume I was some drunk chick, and continue to walk on.

I thought, I just need to make it to the train station, where there would be people to help. I eventually made it to the barriers and stumbled into the toilet. I had vomited more and now was struggling to breathe. I managed to wash my face and then a group of protective service officers greeted me as I walked out of the bathroom. I was asked if I was ok. I was finding it hard to breathe, and struggled to say food allergies. Soon an ambulance was called. It felt like hours, when it was really just minutes. Suddenly, everything went dark and I had stopped fighting to breathe. All the chaos around me disappeared, and I had felt such a strong sense of peace. I felt calm, then suddenly, wham. I was brought back to life. I started to splutter and was placed on a stretcher to go to the hospital. I felt a warmness in my tights, and realised in amongst all the not breathing that I had pooped in my tights. That was the last of my worries, the most important part was the staying alive and breathing part.

When I arrived at the hospital, I was stripped off. The nurse had taken off my tights and she was so calm, even with the strong odour and excrement. I felt ashamed, but I was unable to clean myself. I had to leave my wellbeing to a group of experts, whose focus was on making me join the living once again. In that moment, I had so much respect for the nurses and doctors who put such an effort into making me better.

It was a long night. I felt like a human experiment, I had all these wires attached and an asthma ventilator machine hooked up to me. But I was gradually getting better. I was looking forward to going home and cuddling my dog.

The next morning, I asked the nurses if I could have a towel so I could have a shower to make me feel a little more human. I felt so grateful to clean away the nights' dramas, and wash all the dried blood off my body.

I also managed to wash a little bit of blood out of my outfit using the hand soap, so I at least looked decent. I felt a little shell shocked. I wanted to get changed into something that I didn't nearly die in. I was anticipating getting out of the hospital into the real world.

The doctor finally arrived and said I was free to go. It felt weird walking through the doors and feeling the cool breeze gently caressing my legs. I felt somewhat surreal, I didn't know where I was and how to get to the station.

This was a part of the area that I didn't know. I had to follow signs and ask for help from strangers to get back to the station.

While walking, I had discovered a Kmart, and bought an entire outfit. I was amazed you could buy so much with so little, and I felt better to be out of the clothes that were still stained with blood.

I felt better and didn't want to dwell on my near-death experience. I was due to work at the MCG that day, and decided to work. I didn't want to think how close to death I was, and wanted to just go and live my life. I was a little dazed, and lucky at that time I was able to borrow a uniform so I could work.

Lucky, at that stage security wasn't too tough, they didn't ask for me to open the medical bag full of my dirty clothing. I would have been embarrassed if they did. On reflection, I can't believe that I managed to work a whole shift with a big smile on my face. The human body can be so amazing. You can put your body through so much. You forget how fragile you can be.

I think my most important lesson from this experience is to look beyond stereotypes. Sometimes what you see is not the whole picture. A few months after my near-death experience, I saw this young lady vomiting at the train station. I heard these two boys make fun of her and they decided to video her most fragile state and upload this video to social media. My heart broke, and I wish these boys thought before they posted this video for many people to see. This moment was not entertainment. Sure, she may have been drunk, but just like me she may have had food allergies and vomiting was the side effect. Either way, this moment was private. She needed help just like me. Let a person have her dignity, so she can continue being part of this world. I honestly think I had a guardian angel that day who lead my way to safety. I wasn't ready to leave the earth, I wanted to accomplish so much in my life, and I felt I was just at the tip of how I could make my mark.

Chapter 19
The Dream of Travelling the World

**Lesson: If barriers are blocking your dreams.
Find another way. Break down that door your own way.**

I've always had a full diary, with different casual jobs highlighted, so I know exactly where I'm going. Even though there was one stage where I was juggling so much, that I wore the wrong uniform to the wrong venue! Lucky, it was one of my jobs that had a wardrobe department. I am so grateful that I have the ability to be hired across a diverse range of platforms.

One of my big dreams was to travel the world, and I randomly received an Instagram message from the Winston Churchill Fellowship. I had never heard about this fellowship, that enabled Australians to travel overseas to connect with like-minded people.

Instantly, I wanted to apply. I was curious to see what other people were doing to connect young and older generations. I was amazed to see some great work done overseas in Europe and the United States.

I went to an information session for the Winston Churchill Fellowship at Melbourne University to find out more. Listening to previous winners of the fellowship inspired me to apply and see how far I could go.

Luckily, at the time, Jenna (one of my volunteers) was very skilled at writing and she helped to make sure the application flowed well. I had also asked my old lecturer from Griffith University, Prof. Stephen Stockwell, and Dr. Diana Bossio from Swinburne University, to provide references.

The story of how I met Diana was quite funny. I was looking for journalism students to write stories for the Celebrate Living History website, and decided to have a look on Twitter to do an out-of-the-box search. I stumbled across Dr. Bossio, a lecturer in journalism at Swinburne University. I thought, She looks friendly, and decided to email her and see if she would be open for a chat.

We organised a face-to-face meeting and within a few days, I had journalism students eager to document stories of their relatives, friends and seniors in the community. It was pretty cool to have journalism interns from both Griffith University and Swinburne University representing Celebrate Living History.

It took a few months to create the application for the Winston Churchill Fellowship. While the word count was small, this still made the application difficult. I had to succinctly keep my passion to explore the world, and studying a topic that I love, to as few words as possible, and have a straight-to-the-point attitude to appeal to the judges.

When I finally pressed the submit button on the Winston Churchill Fellowship website, I felt a massive sense of achievement. I wanted fireworks to come out of the computer. Instead, I did a happy dance with my dog, Ava, in my pyjamas.

I loved the whole process of applying for the Winston Churchill Fellowship. The application gave me an opportunity to connect with others doing amazing work with both young and old generations in the United States and Europe. Even though they were so far away, I was inspired by their work, making people smile on the other side of the world. I honestly wanted to incorporate some of their energy into the work I do with Celebrate Living History.

A few months later, I heard back from the Winston Churchill Fellowship. After all that effort, I didn't even get to the second stage.

I was absolutely devastated, and I felt like my heart was broken in half. All that work and effort down the drain.

Then I realised my fate was literally in my own hands. I could either wallow in my self-pity or find a way to still meet these people who had inspired me.

I needed money, and that meant finding a full-time job, which could provide the funds to travel to the United States, where the bulk of the organisations and individuals I had connected with resided.

With Grandma Cissy- Colne England

Celebrate Living History News story. Channel 7 Making a Difference with Kay McGrath. Griffith University Gold Coast Thursday 5 June 2014 Jamie-Lee Dwyer, Bram and Marina Nicolson, Mischeline King, Kay McGrath, Bev

Melbourne Cup Day Flemington Racecourse

Celebrate Living History- Swinburne University O-Week with Melissa Haber

Enjoying a day off work at Mt Buller

Forget About Ages Tour- Bev with artist, Meagan Jain. Workshop held at Adult Day of Dunwoody Atlanta

Forget About Ages Tour- Milwaukee Eagle

Forget About Ages Tour-Duke University, North Carolina. Bev with Education Assistant for the Reflections Program, Brittany Halberstadt, and Director of Education for the Nasher Museum of Art Jessica Kay Ruhle

Hanging with Ava Dognar my mascot

Gold Coast Indy 300

Ride Operator at Drayton Manor UK

Luna Park Melbourne-Filming of Secret Life of Us with actress Deborah Mailman

Entrepreneurs: Generations Apart

Operating Rides at Dreamworld

Luna Park Melbourne- Kate Hart, Delta Goodrum and Bev Wilkinson

Chapter 20
Back to Studies

**Lesson: Enjoy the moment.
Find pleasure in the small things in life.**

At that moment, I was grateful I had gained a Certificate III in Aged Care. I thought having this qualification would be handy for Celebrate Living History, as I would know firsthand what it was like in an aged care home.

For the Certificate III in Aged Care course, I had to complete 120 hours of practical training at an aged care facility. This was one of the hardest moments in my life, it was very different seeing a senior who has great recollection, in comparison to seniors in a nursing home who can only remember fragments and are often frail and vulnerable.

I remember my first day at the Aged Care facility, I was introduced to Amy, who had been working as a personal carer since she was 17 years old.

My first day was mainly observation. In a way, I felt very overwhelmed, like I had dived off the deep end, when I should have really been in the paddling pool. I felt very awkward observing a shower, like I was breaking a barrier of privacy. But it was good to see Amy's technique showering a resident, such as using the Princess Chair so the resident could sit while having a shower hose wash the day's dirt away.

It was a mad rush in the mornings, from 7–8 am all the residents had to be ready for breakfast. Amy was a very fast and efficient worker, and the residents were very lucky to have her look after them. It takes a very special person to work in an aged care home. You have to be compassionate, but at the same time make sure you are efficient, so that all residents can be clean and take on the day.

To be honest, those 120 hours were really difficult at times to complete. I had come in expecting to have moments where I could just relax and have a simple chat with residents. But those moments were brief in a high care nursing home. Every moment was flat out, sometimes personal care could take over an hour for a high needs resident. Some residents were in such pain, but still were very intelligent. They had led such interesting lives, but were now in a nursing home, screaming that every move hurt.

One resident that I dreaded assisting with personal care ended up becoming one of my favourite people to hang out with.

She had led such an interesting life; she was one of the first woman engineers to break into a male dominated world. When I was helping her, I could not help but smile and look at the photos of her on the wall, showing parts of her life that were beyond the nursing home. It made me sad though, that a woman with so much brilliance in her life was stuck inside a body that ached so much. It struck me that getting older can be so hard. You can be young on the inside but your outside shows the passage of time. All that you have achieved and all that you have done, hidden inside a body that is slowly waiting to greet the afterlife. If I had not taken the time to get to know her, all I would see was an older lady in pain, and she was much more than that.

I felt sad that I could not take off the student robe and put on the Celebrate Living History hat to document her story. But I had to be professional, and needed to complete my hours for the Aged Care course. Her story inspires me every day to look beyond the person, and delve inside to discover amazing colour to a life.

There were moments that I will always look fondly back on. One resident was vision impaired, so she took your head into her hands and lightly put her hands over your face. It was such a tender moment. After touching your face, she would say, 'You're just lovely.'

It was so funny, some of the situations I found myself in. One of these moments started as a usual breakfast delivery to one of my favourite residents. I knocked on the door and said, 'Breakfast time.' I found my favourite resident calmly sitting in the chair watching TV. I had set up her food tray when all of a sudden, the food comes crashing down. Mashed egg, porridge and bread, making a huge splat on the floor.

She had jumped up like a spider had snuck into one of her stockings, with a look of pure fright.

I asked what was wrong, she replied, 'I can't eat this food! Someone stole my dentures!'

I said, 'Really? Who would be such a thief!' And then I walked into the bathroom and found her dentures safe and sound on the bench. There was no denture thief, she just forgot where she left them!

Sometimes I let my personality shine through, it was hard to just be clinical and focus on personal care. One time I was showering a resident, and to her amusement, I started rapping, saying, 'Yo, it's Tilly, we in the shower. You got your dope incontinent pad and I have no idea where it goes. Maybe it goes this way, maybe it goes that way.'

Working with other aged care students was often hard. One of my fellow students called a resident a naughty little boy because he likes to wander through the nursing home. I thought it was such a shame that this student didn't get the time to get to know him. This was the same man who I had discussed the morning news with. He was very intelligent, and sometimes he forgot where he was, but still should have been respected much more. Other students called residents darling and sweetie, and I found that really awful. These residents have names and need to be spoken to on a much more human level. These residents are not children, they deserve the respect of having lived a long and fruitful life.

Another resident I assisted with in the lunchroom would give me advice that I always take to heart: 'You can have all the money in the world, but if you are not happy, you can be the most miserable person on earth. Money is not everything, happiness is.'

During my placement at the nursing home, I was surrounded by residents who at first, I felt sorry for. But then I got to know these residents. Some of the residents, despite their position, kept a bright outlook on life; it is the small things that count, from being able to stroke your cat every day to that cheeky extra slice of pizza. It's about being in the moment and appreciating what you have.

Sometimes I felt like I had stepped back in time. Even though these residents may have been many years older than me, they had a certain vulnerability, similar to that of a young child. Time rewinds and stands still when you reach a certain point in life. When caring for some of these residents, I felt like I had a glimpse into what they were like as children, when they smiled and lit up over the simplest things; into that inner vulnerability, when it's a struggle to button up a blouse or brush their teeth. Suddenly, I am the person they depend on, to live their everyday life. And that's scary and beautiful at the same time. I liked to look at the photos on the wall of their rooms, and it's a reminder to look beyond just the person I see, but to remember that they have lived and done wonderful things. Life is really quite fleeting.

After completing my hours at the aged care home, I had grown such a respect for those in the industry. They work so hard and have such big hearts. I know for me it was such a good experience to see life on the other side of a nursing home from an insider's perspective. But I knew that I was not destined to work in a nursing home long-term. I wanted to tell their stories and continue to be an advocate for older people, who are often overlooked in society.

Chapter 21
The Full-Time Job

Lesson: Have faith in yourself. You are more capable than you believe you are. Just try your very best.

After graduating, I had stumbled across an advertisement in the local paper, asking for disability workers with a certificate in aged care. I decided to go to the information session and apply for the role of disability support.

The information session was not too daunting. It was held in one of the houses which they had converted into a staff office. I was nervous, but my friend who worked there was also in the same room, being my cheerleader and passing little notes to me, such as, *This will be good for you. The money is great.*

While I was listening to the presentation about what the job would involve, I became a little anxious. In my head I was thinking, Can I do this job affectively without being scared of bodily fluids? I decided in the end, that while this job seemed like hard work, I was willing to find any way to fund my trip to the United States.

I was scared while I had changed incontinence pads at the nursing home. I didn't feel like I had the stomach to do this in a full-time role. I looked calm and collected but I was really sniffing my collar which I had dabbled with tea tree oil to take away the strong odour.

Luckily, despite my reservations, I got the job in disability care thanks to my friend's great reference. The job turned out to be different than I expected.

For my first shift, all I had to do was sit in the office and read files on the clients. This only made me more doubtful about the job.

The Full-Time Job

The clients I was reading about were involved in car incidents that affected their mental state. Was I really the best person for this job? I was pretty nervous to meet the clients, and felt like I had to study the files inside and out.

Finally, I was paired up with one of the clients. She turned out to be ok to talk to, it wasn't too bad. All I had to do was keep her company and take her shopping. Sure thing, I can do this!

The job turned out to be much harder than I expected. The client loved to walk everywhere, and she was so fast! When she was on a mission, she didn't care who was with her. One time, she was on a mission to get some alcohol. She kept muttering, 'I need a drink; I need a drink.' Next thing you know, we are on the bus where we got off to buy alcohol. I was absolutely flustered. I didn't want to lose her on my second shift, so I had to tag along with her. I was so glad we got back to work safe and sound.

Another client was the polar opposite. He was so lovely, and I absolutely loved spending time with him and his dog. All I had to do was help clean his house and take him out to lunch.

There was one time though, when he forgot his medication. I was so surprised how his personality changed from a sweet man to someone who was very verbally abusive. I was amazed at how one little white pill can make so much difference.

When he started becoming verbally aggressive, I became absolutely frozen. My co-worker wanted me to be his back-up, but I couldn't move. I was stuck in my tracks and hid. Maybe I should have handled the situation differently, and been braver. But you know those times when you fear for your safety? That was one of the times. My co-worker complained about me and I felt so guilty. Now, looking back, I should have felt safe to talk about my feelings but at the time I held a deep sense of shame that I could not handle the man that I had become so accustomed to.

Another time we were trapped inside the office when, all of a sudden, we were surrounded by our client's family members.

She had told her family that we had her money and we were not giving her any. We were on lockdown when her family kept banging on the doors, asking for money. We ended up calling the police, who ushered her family off the premises. It took me a long time to feel safe again on the job after that experience, I was always looking behind my shoulder, ready to bolt to safety if I had to.

There was one shift which involved sleeping overnight in the office. If the client buzzed more than three times during the night, you got paid the normal rate. If they didn't, you only got paid for three hours. There was one stage where all my shifts were sleep-over shifts. I was getting really annoyed, as you never really know if you would get paid more than three hours. A person can't live, or even save, from just these shifts. I soon stopped complaining when I was buzzed more than three times and I walked over to the client's house and opened the door, to see that he had soiled himself and it was like the whole apartment was coated in poo.

I had to remain calm and act like it was no big deal, so that the client would not feel bad. There wasn't enough tea tree oil in the collar of my shirt to cover the smell. I had to mentally block out the smell, and start giving personal care the client, and then move to cleaning the rest of the apartment. It was a long night, and I felt somewhat traumatised at the end of the shift. But I had made it! I had done personal care for the client and his house looked spotless.

I didn't mind active nights, as they were often very quiet. Most nights, all I had to do was deliver medication and do some paperwork. I had to walk around the complex and make sure all the clients were safe and secure for the night. Then I could just relax and read a book while waiting for 6 am to roll around. I wrote in quite a few journals, and enjoyed the early mornings.

After an active night, I would find it hard to wind down and fall asleep. I would often go to a salt room session at the gym, and if my favourite yoga class was on, I would join in. Afterwards, I would prepare my bed for sleep by spraying lavender everywhere, rolling down the blinds, and putting a lavender pillow on my eyes to block out the light. Then I was finally ready to snooze in the daylight hours.

I honestly learned to look beyond the detailed notes in the client's reports. In one of the reports, there was a warning that the client only wanted male carers. My colleague invited me over to the client's house where he was the main carer. I was a bit nervous when I walked through the doors. I was expecting to be yelled out because of my gender. But the client was very calm and was happy to show me his vegetable garden. I loved that he was self-sufficient and lived off his produce, rather than having to go to a supermarket to buy everyday fruit and vegetables. He showed me how he plants avocado seeds and it was amazing to see how one little seed can sprout so many avocados to be enjoyed by him and his family.

This job made me much stronger as a person, with the role including tasks that I never thought I would be capable of. Ironically enough, I'm scared of bodily fluids and I was working in the disability care industry. When it came to compulsory training, we had to learn how to change a stoma bag, which is pouch connected to the abdomen in order to divert the flow of faeces or urine from the bowel or bladder. The waste is then collected in the stoma bag, which can then be discarded. I was dreading this training; I was scared that I would faint. I had looked at YouTube videos prior to the training, and I was dreading every single moment. When I walked into the office, I felt nervous, like I would be caught out as not being a competent disability care worker. I don't know what I was expecting, maybe a mannequin where we would practice with the stoma bag and fake fluids would spill all over the floor. When I sat down, I did the fake-it-until-I-make-it smile and waited, praying that I would not turn white and faint. Our trainer talked a little bit about the reasons why someone would have a stoma bag, and then showed a video on daily life with a stoma bag. It wasn't too bad, I had built up all this anxiety when there was nothing to fear. It wasn't hands-on training, which I was glad about. If we wanted to be ticked off as competent, we would have to change a stoma bag of one of our clients three times. Not surprisingly,

I stayed away from that role! I was fine with just theory and no practice. I was scared that I would do something wrong and cause the client pain, and that would be so horrible.

There was a stage when the clients started getting picky about who would look after them. There were so many shifts to fill, but the current staff pool was not enough. Soon, the company started employing agency workers by the dozen, which meant that I wasn't getting any work even though I was hired by the company. Every day there was a new face, and I lost track of who everyone was. Some of the staff members were welcoming to the agency staff, while some let the agency staff in and didn't make them feel welcomed. The agency staff just sat in the office for the rest of the shift, confused about what exactly they needed to do. When I was on shift, I always made sure the agency staff felt welcomed and I took them on a tour of the homes. I introduced the agency staff to some of the clients who would not mind having some company over. I felt if someone had employed me, and not have given me an orientation or even a briefing of what I would need to do, that I would feel very awkward and my experience would not have been of value.

I think the worst part about the job wasn't the clients, it was more the staff environment. Maybe because we were in such a small space together, this breeds the background for bullying.

There was a certain pecking order. Being a casual meant I was last on the list for work. I wasn't permanent, so I wasn't entitled to write my availability to work.

Maybe I was cheeky, but when the main boss took time off during the holiday period, I saw my opportunity to put my name in the book. Seriously, what is the point in hiring people if you don't give them shifts?

I needed money for America, and I got away with putting my name in the book for a while, until one of the staff members cracked a stink. She was looking through the book and started complaining about me while I could hear her loud and clear.

I felt so awkward and there was no escape. I was stuck in the back room. If I made a noise, she would hear me. I felt like crying. I didn't mean to cause waves, I just wanted shifts to make my dream a reality. It was such a horrible situation to be in, and if I didn't have that goal of going to America I would have quit.

The next day I was asked to purchase liquid paper, which was used ironically to wipe my name off shifts. I was so disappointed that now I would struggle to continue to save for the USA.

But luckily, by that stage, I had saved enough for accommodation, insurance and flights. All I needed was spending money for food, souvenirs, transport and emergencies.

Chapter 22
Side Gig as an Activity Coordinator
Lesson: Think out of the box. Respect those you work with.

At the time, I was also working as an activity coordinator at the local neighbourhood house. That was such a fun job, I loved working with my small group and every week we would go somewhere in the community for lunch.

I really enjoyed bringing in the Herald Sun every morning, and going through news of the day with those in the group.

Particularly, in the star signs section, I would pretend to be a psychic and wrap a scarf around my face looking mysterious. Then in a wistful voice go through the week's predictions with the group. We would always end up giggling because I looked so silly!

I got to have a lot of fun implementing out-of-the-box activities. Once I ran a meditation session, where I told everyone to close their eyes while playing relaxing music. One of the clients kept opening his eyes and looking at me. It was so hard to suppress my giggles, especially when I was putting on the calm, relaxing voice.

I also did regular activities, like Hangman, mainly because I liked drawing on the whiteboard. My hangman would not just be a stick figure, but would have features like a big smile on his face. And clothes on his body! I didn't like a cold hangman!

I would always find a way to add a twist to an activity, to ease boredom and to make my group members guess what was happening next.

Sometimes this role was difficult. There was a stage where one of my group members had his father in hospital. His father was in palliative care, and was not long for this world. I felt so sorry for him, but he kept on disrupting the group every couple of minutes to call the hospital. He was in pain and I was not sure how I could help him. Luckily, there was another coordinator who could lead the group while I escorted him outside to make his phone calls. It was hard. He was 36 years old but, in his mind, he was only 10 years old. He had the vulnerability of a child, in an adult's body. All I could do was to try and keep his mind on other things. And I was glad when his mother came around to take him home, he was not ready to be in a social group. All he had on his mind was his father, and the group was not a good distraction.

Every month, we would have a special guest visit the community group. I loved these moments, as it was an opportunity to learn something different and have a little bit of fun with the group. One month, we had a teacher who conducts exercises for those that have difficulty moving. One of my clients wanted to participate, even though these activities had the potential to be hard for him. My co-worker said, 'It is ok, just sit if it's too hard.'

He replied, 'No, it is ok. I can do it.' With a little bit of assistance, he thrived. He did so well. He was determined that despite his disability, he could do anything. The mind is really quite powerful. If you believe you can do anything, then you will find away. He blew me away every time, so that I didn't see his disability, just the person he was. Truly amazing. Despite adversity, you can do anything. You just have to believe you can do it.

One of the group members was 98 years old, and she loved to wear this beautiful red cardigan that she made for her mum in her final days. The cardigan was so intricate and took hours of hand knitting to complete. I realised that clothing can be a work of art, and if made well, these clothes can be passed down through the generations. I felt sad that in today's world, our clothes are made on such a huge scale, being produced for the masses. We have lost that sense of craftwork that can be passed through generations.

The lessons that I leaned from this job were valuable. One of my group members had trouble speaking, but when he held a violin, it was like magic. Suddenly, he was happy and in his element. All barriers were down, and this sweet sound filled the air. It's really amazing how the power of an instrument can transform an individual. Sometimes the most talented people are those that you don't notice. Then, suddenly, they take you by surprise in the most beautiful way.

I was pretty sad when they found a replacement for my role. It was pretty hard having to be interviewed for the position, even though I knew at the start that I was a fill-in and I was only temporary.

The person that interviewed me was fairly new to the position, and she wanted to shake things up. And that meant new staff members.

When I was with her, I felt like she was always looking for something wrong. The way I did the activities was too boring for her. I felt like I wasn't good enough. It was most likely a good thing she didn't choose me to continue working alongside her. I would have become quite anxious, and second guessed the activities I was running.

I remember one activity to shake things up was a make-a-pizza day. It was fine in theory, but this activity was run on a steaming hot day. I felt sorry for the volunteers assisting, they went above and beyond what was expected.

When there was extra pizza, my co-worker didn't offer the pizza to the volunteers, which I thought was rude. I ended up giving the volunteers the pizza, and apologising for the hot working conditions.

Later on, she would get fired for bullying another team member. The social group is no longer running, which is a shame, as it felt like such a close-knit family that enjoyed getting together for a good chat.

Chapter 23
Lift Off of the Forget About Ages Tour

Lesson: Surround yourself with people who are passionate about what they do. Their magic may just rub off on you!

It took a year for all my hard work to pay off. All those long hours and the job juggling made the *Forget About Ages* tour a reality. This tour was one that I had dreamt of since I had created an application for the Winston Churchill Fellowship. I remember feeling absolutely devastated that my application, to learn from organisations and people focused on programs connecting young people and seniors in the United States, was unsuccessful. But this rejection had stirred something inside me. I was determined to make my own way, and to make this journey a reality. This journey was a huge itinerary that saw me travel every few days to a different state in the United States.

Finally, I was going on the *Forget About Ages* tour that I had created through saving hard and running a small crowd funding project. I was very lucky that my co-workers at the Melbourne Cricket Club supported me on this journey. In exchange for small gifts that I scored while volunteering for Business Chicks, their donations towards this huge journey flooded in.

When it came time to depart for the United States, I could not believe I was really going. My mum travelled with me into the city and bid me farewell at the Skybus terminal. This was really happening! I had to pinch myself. I was going to the United States again, on the tour of my dreams.

It felt weird going through to the international terminal and going through security. This was not a simple trip to the Gold Coast, I was going international. I was going on a huge Qantas airplane to the other side of the world.

When I stepped onto the tarmac, it felt surreal. I really could not believe I was going. It hit me when I was seated, and looking down at the clouds, saying *Goodbye* to Melbourne for a little while.

It was such a long flight. I was grateful for the stopover in Auckland, it was so great to stretch my legs. I was stuck in the middle seat, and the man next to me didn't move a lot. Meanwhile, I was the polar opposite, I liked to move my legs and most importantly be able to go to the bathroom without worrying about squeezing between people. I ended up spending most of the flight chatting to the stewards at the back of the plane, taking in the magnificent views of the skyline. It was much easier than staying in my seat.

After 15 hours of flying, I finally touched down in Los Angeles. I was tired and disoriented but excited that I was finally in the United States.

Going through customs felt like I was in a herd of cattle, being prodded to move forward. I double checked before going into the line that I didn't have any fruit on me! I saw the cutest security dog, but I knew if he sat beside me, I was in big trouble! Border Security is one of my favourite shows, and I've seen what happens if you do bring some fruit into another country!

Finally, a few hours later, after collecting my bags, I had to scope out ways to get to Podshare, where I would be staying a few nights before going to New York. It was overwhelming when I left the terminal. There were men asking around to see if anyone needed a lift anywhere. I remember being suspicious, as I had just arrived and thought their prices might be ridiculously high to take advantage of tourists.

So, I opted to take a shuttle bus to my accommodation in downtown Hollywood. I had seen Podshare featured in a Buzzfeed video, and thought it was pretty cool. Podshare was not only a bed for the night but a co-working space for entrepreneurs. I thought, what a good way to start my tour, with creative people who think outside the square.

I eventually made it to Podshare, where I literally checked in and crashed on the bed. I was pretty jetlagged from all that travel, even though it was weird having people work on their computers in the common area while I snored. There wasn't much privacy, so they could see a very tired Australian sprawled over the bed!

Eventually I woke up and trotted around Hollywood. It was so cool to be walking distance from the famous Hollywood boulevard. I posed with the handprints of my favourite Hollywood stars. Then, I ventured out to find essential food and a soy latte!

One of my highlights was going out to dinner with my new Podshare friends. Belle, one of the interns, invited me out for Mexican food, and it was so lovely just to be surrounded by people passionate about what they do for a living. This also sparked an obsession with Mexican food. From that moment, I would have Mexican food on a regular basis. The servings were so big that I could save money by eating half a meal and saving the rest for the next day.

It was so strange to be on holiday but still have to organise plans for the next few weeks. I spent a few hours using my Skype credit to finalise my interview with the nonnas at Enoteca Maria, a restaurant in Straten Island that hires grandmas as chefs. I had an option of interviewing the nonnas from Macedonia, or from Italy. Because I was worried that the language barrier would be hard to overcome, I had to reorganise my schedule to fit around the Italian nonnas. While it may seem silly, initially, interviewing the Italian nonnas clashed with my *Gossip Girl* tour that I had organised months prior. I am a huge fan of *Gossip Girl*, and I would have been devastated if I missed the tour. The session I wanted to change to was booked out online. So, I made a call to the *Gossip Girl* tour office to plead my case. I even threw in the, 'This tour has been on my bucket list for so long, and I've travelled so far,' line. Luckily, someone had pulled out and I took their spot.

Chapter 24
New York

Lesson: Don't be nervous. Travel and meet people. Enjoy their stories.

The flight to New York was daunting! Even though I had arrived early, they were not able to allocate my seat. So, I had to wait inside the terminal while others boarded my flight. They had a waiting list for others, patiently waiting for people to pull out, as there is an incentive to save money on travel costs. I remember looking at another Australian who was also concerned about not being able to board the flight. Somehow, she snuck through and encouraged me to do the same. However, I was stopped and told to wait. Eventually I was placed in a seat next to the toilet! Even though at times the smells would waft out, I was grateful I was on the flight.

If I had missed the flight, it would have created a domino effect. I was on a tight schedule, interviewing people and travelling to a new city every day. One wrong turn and my flights, accommodation and meetings would go down the drain. My biggest fear was that all the organisation and saving money would have been for nothing. This was no ordinary holiday, this was me, making my research dream come true.

Six hours later, I had arrived in New York! Even though this was the second time I had visited the city, it didn't cease to amaze me how busy and vibrant the city was.

I took a shuttle bus to my hostel, which was in the middle of all the excitement, close to Central Park. Even though I was on a tight budget, I was in a premium location with free breakfast every day.

At the hostel, it felt like a clash of worlds. The new generation of CCUSA counsellors were also staying at the hostel. Some of the counsellors had never left their home country and this was the first time they had hit international soil. They huddled together, chatting about where in the USA they were headed and what they were teaching. I remember missing that excitement of making new friends that would last a lifetime. That certainty you will have someone to travel with for the rest of your stay. I felt a bit sad that I was embarking on this trip alone, but confident that I was doing the right thing. I wanted to inspire others to dream big, and despite facing barriers, to make their goals happen. I truly believe you are the master of your own destiny. No one but you can make things happen.

I remember my first subway trip being quite daunting. While walking to the station, I witnessed a man having a wee on a car. I didn't know what to do. So, I looked the other way. I felt sorry for the owner of the car. Whatever that person did, it must have been really bad for that man to wee on the car!

I was so excited to see what the life my favourite characters, Serena Van der Woodsen and Blair Waldorf, would have been like, on the famous *Gossip Girl* tour. My old housemate, Jesse, would have been so jealous. We used to watch back-to-back episodes of *Gossip Girl* on the Gold Coast, and we just loved the drama and the thrill of what was going to happen next. At that time, I wished he was there with me, giggling away and happily pointing at all the familiar locations. My favourite location was the iconic Grand Central Station in Midtown Manhattan. Nothing beats the beautiful architecture through this transport hub. What I found really fascinating was the cathedral-like main concourse ceiling, where there are 12 constellations printed in gold leaf, plus 2500 stars with 59 LED stars twinkling their way through the ceiling.

I loved that you could also have a glimpse of what the ceiling was like before it was cleaned, with a small dark patch of brick revealing what the ceiling looked like before it was closed for restoration in the 1990s. This little brick shows the 70 percent coverage of nicotine and tar from cigarettes when smoking was allowed in the building, way before it become unacceptable to smoke in public places. I like to imagine all the people dressed in their finest outfits, gossiping, many years ago under this ceiling. With some oozing Hollywood glamour, mingling and smoking, just like Audrey Hepburn, unaware of the health risks this simple act would create in the future.

My favourite *Gossip Girl* episode was when Blair and Serena stole clothes from a fashion shoot and galivanted all over Manhattan, taking photos and bonding with each other. I just loved their simple joy, taking photos of these bright, colourful outfits at iconic locations, such as at a giant fountain at Central Park. It was fun to see where these episodes were shot, and to imagine my best friend and I wearing loud outfits and simply just enjoying being in the moment of a random fashion shoot.

There weren't many solo travellers on the *Gossip Girl* tour bus, it was mostly young girls with their mums! I didn't care though, and made friends who took photos of me all over New York. I didn't just want selfies on this trip, but genuine photos that I could look back on and smile. Sometimes it was tempting to just do selfies, but I missed the experience of getting to know a stranger and of having conversations that ordinarily would not evolve if I had stayed in my own little bubble.

After the tour, I decided to walk through Central Park. It was so beautiful, and all the trees were out in bloom. I didn't feel unsafe as I was surrounded by people. While walking on the footpath, out of the corner of my eye, I spotted an ice cream truck. I love the music that blares out of ice cream trucks, these simple tunes make me think of my childhood. It was such a nice afternoon that I had to spoil myself with an ice cream sandwich. Nothing makes the day better than an ice cream!

Soon, the next day arrived, and it was time to travel to Enoteca Maria in Staten Island. I was worried about getting lost in the subway!

After writing myself step by step instructions, I managed to make it to South Ferry Station, and from there I was to catch a ferry to St George.

Suddenly, I was herded with a bunch of tourists, who were keen to see the statue of Liberty. I explained a few times that I was wanting to catch the St George ferry to see the nonnas at Enoteca Maria. Everyone I spoke to looked at me, heard my accent, and just assumed I was one of the tourist group. I suppose it's a strange request, wanting to go on a local ferry. Eventually, I made it onto the free ferry to St George. I think if you want a low-cost alternative to seeing the Statue of Liberty, this is a great way to do so! I could still see the Statue of Liberty, even though she was a fair distance away. After the interview, I did decide to join the tourists and meet the Lady of Liberty in the flesh.

I ended up being an hour early for the interview, so I ended up pottering around St George. It's a nice little town. I bought some snacks and sat on the library stairs, and drew some of the people that I had seen on public transport. Just for something different, I drew people located in all the places I had visited in the United States. In a way, it was like a unique journal, and depicted the different styles and cultures of each city.

Drawing for me is a way to take time out to do something that's not only creative but fun. As a child, I would always get in trouble during mathematics class. I would look like I was working on equations, but I was actually drawing people. I found mathematics to be really boring, so drawing eased the boredom. I got to play in my own little world, drawing people that I was yet to meet. Needless to say, my grades in mathematics were very low!

Finally, it was time to meet Joe Scaravella, the owner of Enoteca Maria, and the Italian nonnas, Adelina V. and Christina Carrozza. It was so funny, I was so nervous that I would lose the footage of this interview that I used two cameras.

One was my Samsung video phone, and the other my small handheld camera. I was prepared for all emergencies! To prop up the cameras, we used both plates and boxes!

Despite not having a professional camera crew, I was able to capture all three interviews well.

When I interviewed Adelina, there were some language barriers. I struggled to ask questions that were easy to answer, but we got there in the end. Adelina's passion for food and cooking for her family shone through!

The interview with Christina went well! She loved my Australian accent and was curious about why I had come to America. I told her after seeing a documentary on the nonnas, I really wanted to see in person how Joe runs the restaurant, and meet the nonnas who share their home cooked foods with the community.

I thought it was a beautiful thing to share these traditional cooking skills with younger generations as well.

Looking back, I wasn't your ordinary TV crew or journalist. I was really just a person who wanted to be inspired, and meeting the nonnas and Joe made me so happy. It felt so good to say, 'I'm interviewing on behalf of Celebrate Living History,' and to gain the respect of representing a media organisation. Even though this media organisation was one that I created!

It's funny, I had totally forgotten to book a shuttle bus to catch my flight at LaGuardia airport to North Carolina. I was too obsessed with getting change for the washing machines the night prior. Anyone that knows me understands my need for fresh clean clothes!

After having my breakfast and checking out, I realised I needed a way to get to the airport. Silly me, not thinking in advance! If I missed this flight, my entire itinerary would have collapsed in a domino effect. I had booked accommodation and organised so many meetings. If I had missed one flight, everything would have been buggered up!

In a blind panic, I called up a taxi to give me a lift to the airport. I had this flustered look on my face and the taxi driver said, 'No point in panicking! You miss your flight, you miss your flight. You just book another one.' Luckily, $100 later, I had made it to the airport. Then I found out I was dropped off at the wrong terminal. I literally ran like a crazy woman to the shuttle bus, muttering to myself, *Bloody hell, why is this airport so big? Why do I have such small legs, it's a bloody effort!*

I eventually made it to the correct terminal, and they were just boarding my flight. I thanked my lucky stars that I had made it on time!

I was rewarded with a window seat overlooking the clouds. No matter how many times I fly, I just love feeling like a bird in the sky!

Chapter 25
North Carolina

**Lesson: Don't feel like an imposter.
You are there for a reason. Rock the real you.**

When I arrived in North Carolina, it was so beautiful and lush in comparison to the craziness of New York.

I loved looking at the trees and taking in the fresh air. The Uber driver that picked me up laughed when I kept repeating, 'It's so green! So many trees!'

We finally got to my Airbnb, and my Uber driver was so nice. She waited until I had found the keys and was safely inside. She had warned me not to go walking by myself at night as there are some shady characters.

A few hours later, I met my Airbnb host, Kate, and her cute dog, Sandy. It had been a while since I hung out with a dog, so it was a refreshing surprise. Sandy was so cute and super excited. It's funny, it turned out that Kate worked at Duke University, where I would be attending a museum symposium on art programs that cater to those with Alzheimer's and their care partners.

It is funny, I felt like an imposter when I first hopped on the free shuttle bus from the 21 Museum Hotel in Durham. All the other people were from museums all around the United States, while I was from Australia and represented Celebrate Living History, an organisation that I had made a reality.

It was pretty cool, though, that I was part of this group, as I loved art and working with seniors.

We arrived at Duke University, where I met Education Assistant for the Reflections Program, Brittany Halberstadt, and Director of Education for the Nasher Museum of Art, Jessica Kay Ruhle, who both organised the museum symposium. It was amazing to meet both these ladies in person. Both had worked tirelessly to connect all these museum professionals, and one chick from Australia.

It was pretty cool. The symposium was held at the on-campus museum, the Nasher. It is such a wonderful place, located in the heart of Durham, where the community can be exposed to unique artwork.

The Nasher is surrounded by lush green plants, and it was beautiful to experience art and nature mingling together to create a calm and peaceful environment.

It was a long week of learning about programs that focus on connection between seniors and art. It was amazing to see the passion that all the museum representatives had over creating programs that bond seniors and art in the community. From that symposium, many programs were created to forge these bonds, and it was a privilege to be part of that creative process.

What I really liked about hanging out with such a large group was the opportunity to be social. Travelling on my own could get very lonely, I was experiencing so much but I really had no one to talk to and share my journey with, in person. I missed that part of travelling with someone. But then again, travelling on your own opens you up to new opportunities to meet new people.

One of my highlights of North Carolina was a simple baseball game. I loved seeing the excitement of the locals gathering to see the Durham Bulls play. I would not have gone on my own, mainly because I would have felt silly, but with a small group it was less daunting. It's funny, a game of baseball is similar to the atmosphere of an AFL game at the Melbourne Cricket Ground. I felt instantly comfortable in the crowd, cheering on the Durham Bulls.

I returned to North Carolina a second time to join the newly created *Reflections* program, which was in the pilot stage, and I felt honoured to join the first of their tours. The *Reflections* program is directed at both caregivers and those with Alzheimer's or Dementia who they look after. The *Reflections* program is held at the Nasher Museum, and is aimed at focusing on art in the moment. What was really cool, was that it didn't matter where the art was from. It was about using the imagination to focus on the story. Each tour held a theme and the one I joined was focused on meditation. I loved that we got to delve further into the seaside artwork. Both Brittany and Jessica asked questions such as, 'Does this beach remind you of a certain place?' These questions brought up smiles as the participants thought of their favourite beaches, and the sun and water lapping against their feet. We also were treated to a tai chi and jazz fusion, which was quite relaxing to watch as the jazz player and tai chi expert swayed together.

Chapter 26
Chicago

**Lesson: Embrace strangers. Go on adventures.
You can enjoy concerts solo.**

Next on my tour was Chicago, one of my favourite places in the United States, as I just love the blues culture, and Lake Michigan which sparkles throughout the city. I was very lucky to be in contact with my friend's uncle, Archie, who was a local in Chicago.

Archie met me at my accommodation, Freehand Chicago, which was located in the heart of the city. It was pretty cool accommodation, even though I wasn't looking forward to sharing in a mixed three-person room. Staying in a hostel room can be a mixed bag. You really don't know who you will be sharing with, and hope that the others are not too noisy. Or a bit weird! My last stay in hostel-like accommodation was Podshare in Los Angeles. It was a great location but there was this one guest that went to bed at around 1 am. He would toss and turn and yell out swear words! He wasn't very pleasant to listen to, and there were times I was tempted to put a sock in his mouth to mute the noise. Luckily, this time around there were no issues, except there was this one guest who thought she was meant to be staying in my bunk which made my stay a bit awkward.

She was chatting with her new friends and I was like, 'Well, I think you'd better see the reception staff and they should help you.' There was no way I was moving bunks! All my stuff was there!

Anyway, after getting settled, I met Archie in the reception area, and he showed me around his favourite city.

It was a treat to be in the company of a local so passionate about showing me around. And truth be told, it was nice not to rely on the kindness of strangers to take photos next to major tourist locations, he was happy to take as many photos as he could!

What I love most about Chicago is the architecture. The buildings are made with so much heart and detail. When Archie spoke about the buildings throughout the city, he spoke words that made me feel excited to be surrounded by so much history and craftsmanship. It really is all the little details that craft the heart of the city of Chicago.

Archie showed me Millennium Park, and it was so cool to see so much passion for the blues. At the time, Chicago was hosting The Blues Festival, and I was treated to free concerts. I just loved the energy and vibe that the performers gave off. I wasn't a fan of the blues before Chicago, but I became a big fan after!

Chapter 27
Milwaukee

Lesson: Sometimes the biggest lessons are those you don't expect.

Next on my travels was Milwaukee. This time around was my first trip on a Greyhound bus. I managed to order a Lyft driver to the Greyhound terminal, and it was his first time driving someone. I felt very privileged to be his first passenger, and I hope I inspired him to continue giving lifts to random strangers. I never really thought being a Lyft or Uber driver could be a daunting experience, but every day you are letting new people into your life. Every day there are strangers in your car. You have to leave it to chance that these passengers will behave well. Or, only make yourself available during the day where you are more likely to avoid drunk people coming home after a big night out! All in all, I have depended so much on Uber and Lyft drivers during my travels, and they are often the most friendly people, who can help me get a local's perspective on a new city. Especially in America, it was quite important to know how to get around and what dangerous suburbs to avoid!

When I arrived at the bus depot in Milwaukee, it was a bit daunting. I had messaged my Airbnb host to pick me up. She never replied, and I wasn't sure how to get to my accommodation. Should I walk? It didn't look too far. I was glad I ended up waiting for Janet. The walk to her house, while not too far, was a bit daunting. I stood out like a sore thumb. When I arrived at Janet's Airbnb, it felt like I had stepped back in time. Her house was from the Victorian era, circa the 1800s. When I stepped into the loungeroom, I loved the antique furnishings, and that Christmas was all year round. Even though it was June, Santa was waving cheekily at me. Janet mentioned that some of the houses on the street have ballrooms in them, which was a popular pastime in the past. I can't imagine living in a house where a ballroom was a necessity! What was really welcoming were the abundance of snacks, Janet had these little touches which made travelling on a budget just that little bit easier! After settling in, I decided to explore the neighbourhood. At first, the atmosphere was pretty frightening. I saw people arguing with each other, and a car pulled over, and the driver handed over a suspicious package. I still decided that I wanted to check out the dollar store that I had spotted from the car. So, I decided to brave the streets and make my way to the store. There was no way could I be killed in bright daylight, right? On the way to the store, I spotted this bright piece of street art. An eagle surrounded by beautiful colours, soaring into the skies. Looking at that piece of artwork reminded me of a diamond in the rough. In such a tough neighbourhood, I wasn't expecting this eagle to appear. So brave and full of hope for the future. I realised in that moment the neighbourhood may be tough, but it wasn't too bad. Wherever you go, there will be tough people but there will always be people that think of the bright side and make the world a little bit better. I ended up buying a colourful bracelet from the dollar store to remind me to break down stereotypes and to not always assume the worst of a neighbourhood. It's just like people, if you only look at a person at face value, you may never get to see their unique personality which can be full of flavour. The next day, I had my first day of the Generations United Global Intergenerational Conference, which I had joined as both a delegate and a speaker. It was so cool being there in person, and seeing all the research that I had done for the Winston Churchill Fellowship evolve into the real world.

It was fun to join a tour that involved travelling to communities that incorporate generations of families, connecting over a common activity. For example, a community garden that saw the elders share their love of tending to growing vegetables and fruit, to nourish not only their family but others in the community. I loved seeing the young children and teenagers respect their elders, and follow their instructions to tend lovingly to fruit and vegetables that will nourish not only themselves, but the whole community.

I also really enjoyed seeing the Timeslips program, run by social entrepreneur, Sam Decker, in person at the local retirement village. The Timeslips program involved residents having fun by taking part in mini performances, where it doesn't matter what you remember. You can just see the pure joy the residents have when they say a line and for a moment, they are an actor or actress!

Over the week, I was exposed to so many people who worked with both generations. I loved interacting with so many people from different organisations throughout the United States, and internationally, who were as passionate as I am about connecting people from two very vast generations.

I was excited but nervous to do my mixed-tape speech about Celebrate Living History, in my mind I thought I was going to be on a big stage.

In reality, I was in a conference room with a small audience. I was a bit disappointed, in my mind my imagination took over the scene that I dreamt up, which was full of people clapping and me standing on a red carpet, inspiring people to make my dream a reality.

But I thought, I will do my best, and make my small audience smile. I was last to talk, and it was a tough crowd. It was at the end of the day, and we were all sleepy and ready for a nap.

It came to my time to talk. I was surprisingly still nervous, and my palms were sweating. I was ready to come to the front of the room.

I looked at everyone and thought, This is my playground, and changed my speech on the spot.

I brought up the photo I had taken of the eagle a few days ago, and asked everyone, 'What do you see, when you see this eagle soar above the flames?' and, 'Where do you think this street art is from?'

I decided to make my audience think, and interact with everyone. We had spent so much time sitting and listening to everyone, that it felt like an information overload.

I had a few people yell out fancy areas, like Chicago or New York. And I replied, 'In reality, this eagle is in one of the toughest neighbourhoods in Milwaukee, just a few blocks away.'

I replayed my story of walking through the neighbourhood and feeling scared. But then looking at this Eagle and feeling a sense of security, and that it can't be that bad. For people to create this soaring eagle, there must be some sense of pride and belonging. And the lesson that I learned was to never take things at face value, if you look more closely, you might just be surprised and discover a golden nugget underneath it all.

I looked out at the audience and registered a look of surprise. They were not expecting to be woken up. I loved that I saw a sparkle in their eyes. It may have not been a huge audience, but I felt like this was my calling to be a speaker and to inspire people to think outside the square. The talk was a little bit about Celebrate Living History, but was more of a platform to see if a simple speech can inspire people to take a chance to make their dreams a reality. And I was simply happy that I had the opportunity to do that in front of an international audience. For me, Celebrate Living History started out as a dream, but became much more than that. Celebrate Living History was my saviour, and gave me hope that my skills and talents can mentor a younger generation and remove the invisibility cloak of older generations to the world.

The next talk I gave was at a round table, which involved delegates going around to each table to speak to the organisations and individuals. There were so many tables, and I was hidden towards the back end of the room. I felt kind of sad that not many people came to my table. I had prepared so much but didn't really get the opportunity to share my journey. I had even teared up a little bit and had to wipe my face. All that build up, for very little time. But I cheered myself and wiped away my tears. I had to move on and continue, I didn't come that far to give up.

I had a few delegates come up to me and say, 'It's very difficult in this industry to create a sustainable job,' and that I'd done very well to get this far. Even though they had good intentions, my insides screamed out, I have hope and I believe I can make my dream sustainable. I hadn't come so far to be told to face reality. I took a breath and gave myself a mental pat on the back.

Sometimes it can be hard when you are the only person backing yourself. It's easy to lose faith in your abilities and give into mainstream life. Get a job, makes some babies and retire once you are done. While there is nothing wrong with that life, I wanted more. I wanted to be happy on the creative path that I made. I wanted my personality to shine in the hugest way. And I honestly thought the only person that can make it a reality was myself. If I lost faith, I know that I could easily fall into a pit of depression. That scared me; losing faith in my ability to believe in myself.

Chapter 28

Atlanta

Lesson: Let your imagination soar.

Next on my list was Atlanta, where I would meet artist, Meagan Jain, who I had admired for a long time. She held a successful crowdfunding campaign on Start Some Good, to assist in running the *Ageless Interaction* program, which involved young university students bonding with seniors in care facilities through creating art together. I loved Meagan's passion and compassion for the older generations. She doesn't care about age, just on the person underneath. It was her mission to create a totally ageless community, where age doesn't matter.

When I first met Meagan inside the train station carpark, she had such a presence that was radiating around her. She was tall but not overwhelmingly tall, and her hair was bleached blonde. Her pants were splatted full of paint, showing her love of art for everyone to see. She had this big smile that could have only come from someone living her best life.

I was stunned, and could not believe I was meeting her in person, and helping her in a workshop held at Adult Day of Dunwoody. When I walked into the room, there was this excited chatter between the participants, like they were waiting all day for this moment; to paint and play with colours on canvas.

Meagan showed an example of a flower for everyone to follow. Some of the seniors followed step by step, others just did their own thing. Even having a nap during class!

Meagan sat me next to a senior who had dementia. She soon got bored and started poking the lady next to her. It's funny, when you run these classes you have to think ahead and ensure your participants are seated next to a person that they are compatible with. The lady next to her was incredibly patient and calmed her down. If she sat next to someone who also had dementia, this could have been a recipe for failure!

I tried to help the senior with dementia with her painting, but she was just so excited to have a new person in her class, she could not focus on the task of painting a flower. I ended up putting the brush in her hand and guiding her to create a masterpiece. Meagan told me, 'It's ok if she doesn't want to paint.' I stopped guiding her, and realised while having a painting at the end of the day is a great outcome for the relatives to hang on the wall, that the social interaction was more important. If Meagan didn't run a painting class, this participant most likely would be sitting in the lounge, bored, watching old movies. Most of the seniors followed Meagan' directions. One gentleman ignored Meagan and created his own artwork based on the countryside. I was surprised at how advanced he was. He may have difficulty socialising with others but he was happy in his own world. He let his imagination soar in ways that made you see a glimpse into his personality.

In that class, I realised that through simply painting, a person gets to explore a world where they are totally free to be creative. In a way, painting is an escape from a body that may be in a lot of pain and edging closer to the end of life.

From what I could see, Meagan runs such a great program that makes her personality shine in the hugest way. She was in her element, guiding and leading seniors into creating a painting that may be cherished by their families for many generations to come.

Even though Meagan ran a great class, she struggled trying to raise the price of the program to effectively cover the materials and time. I saw her negotiate with the staff for a higher fee, and pitch a smaller class that would see the seniors really interested in the program get involved and grow their talents. I was impressed with Meagan's ability to be business savvy for her classes to be sustainable long term. She negotiated well and I hope she was successful in being able to raise her fees to cover materials and her talented skills set. It would be a shame if she had to cancel the classes, simply through lack of funding.

After the painting workshop, I joined Meagan for a drink and nachos. It was nice to get to know about her passion for creating murals and art in her local community. I told her that at times I would feel guilty charging people to tell their story, and often write their stories for free. Meagan said I should not be afraid to charge for my skills and abilities, if I wanted to make a living doing what I do best. Her advice made sense. Making a living is a good thing, without it I would continue to struggle, juggling many jobs for years to come.

Meagan was kind enough to write down her favourite things to do in the city. One of the activities I really enjoyed was walking the Beltline, which is two-mile trail which runs between Piedmont Park and Inman Park. I loved the artwork that brought personality to my long walk on the trail. I stopped over at Ponce City market, to enjoy an ice-cream and an icy cold drink. I absolutely loved the architecture, and the way the building felt old school but modern at the same time.

Atlanta was one of my favourite cities, but my Airbnb was located on the outskirts of the city. Every time I reached a new destination, I always asked the host about a safe way to move around the city. My host, Karl, suggested I take an Uber to the train station, as I stood out like a sore thumb. But the thing was, there was a bus stop that was located just outside my accommodation. Being on a budget, I thought, *I need to save money*, and decided to ignore my host and try out the local bus. Karl was right, I stood out on the bus. I was the only person who was not African American, but it turned out to be ok. I loved listening to their colourful talks. It was weird to stand out simply because of the colour of my skin but I understand that for people of colour, standing out in a room and feeling unsafe because of the colour of your skin is a regular experience.

I guess not many Australians travel to Atlanta and catch the local bus! I remember reaching the train station and feeling really anxious about buying a ticket. There was no one in a ticket booth to ask, so I had to trust my gut and ask someone to help. I ended up speaking to people trying to get commuters interested in becoming Mormon. Ordinarily, I would avoid this type of booth, but I needed someone to help and ease my anxiety about catching the train. Travelling on your own makes you really reach outside your comfort zone! I eventually learned how the Atlanta public transport system works, but like everything, it takes time to be really comfortable navigating a new city.

After a few weeks travelling around the United States, it was time to go home. I was sad to leave my adventures behind and join the realities of the real world once again. I had gotten used to packing up every few days and exploring a new city.

Chapter 29
New Zealand

**Lesson: While travelling rely on the kindness of strangers.
They let you use Google Maps on their phone so you don't get lost.**

Before heading home to Melbourne, I made a pit stop in New Zealand. I've always wanted to go to Auckland, and have been fascinated with Maori culture, so it was the perfect way to end the trip.

I landed at Auckland airport at 6 o'clock in the morning, and was feeling the effects of jet lag. My brain wasn't ready to be switched on, but I needed to find a way to reach my hostel for the next few days.

I ended up catching the airport shuttle and getting lost trying to find the YHA hostel. It is funny, you don't realise how attached you are to Google Maps on your phone until you have to rely solely on the kindness of strangers to lead you to your destination. I had a phone, but as I was overseas, there was no way I could connect to the internet unless I had free Wi-Fi!

I eventually made it to the YHA hostel, but I had to wait in the common area for a few hours before my room was free. They let me use the facilities, but it was very difficult navigating a suitcase into the bathroom to have a shower. I spent most of my time apologising for being in the way! I managed to score some free bread from other travellers, and then had a huge nap while waiting. All I wanted was a comfy bed and a cuddle from my dog, Ava.

Eventually, I made it to my hostel room and zonked out. I would later go trotting around Auckland, but for now I needed energy to keep going!

I was really looking forward to checking out the Auckland Museum and indulging my interest in some local culture.

After feeling rested, I went out and most importantly, bought a soy latte! Every day while travelling, I allocated a coffee allowance of one a day! There is something about a perfectly brewed coffee that makes me feel happy to tackle a brand-new day.

Coffee in hand, I made it to the Auckland Museum, which is located on top of a hill with perfect views of the city. I looked out from the hill and thought I was lucky to be able to explore, and discover little gems of this city that I ordinarily would never get the opportunity to.

When I first entered the museum, I was struck by the beautifully-made exhibition celebrating the Maori culture. I absolutely loved the three floors of taonga (treasures) from the Maori people of the Oceania region and New Zealand. A row of portraits of Maori people from various generations stood out. I just loved how powerful and full of strength the people within the pictures looked. How their artwork on their faces displayed pride for their tribes and the sparkle in their eyes represented their love of their community and way of life.

It was a nice way to end my journey, being surrounded by so much love that the Maori culture represented.

During my time in Auckland, a major rugby game was on. I enjoyed the excitement of the city and the people eager to cheer on their teams. Some people even dressed up in their team colours, chanting their theme song in the streets. In that moment, I craved the excitement of the football at the Melbourne Cricket Ground. Nothing beats the roar of the crowd when their favourite team kicks a goal, and the unique bond people have with their chosen team. I also missed my friends at the MCG, who had supported me so much on this journey. I was looking forward to coming home and using this new-found knowledge to do something good in the community.

A week later was my last flight, back home to Melbourne. I was excited to be coming back and unsure what my destiny would have for me. How would I use this knowledge, and who would want to listen to my stories?

When I arrived home, everything felt different, and it was weird to unpack my bag for the last time. I was used to travelling so often, but I was happy to be back and finally get my cuddles from my dog, Ava. It was so funny, it took a week for Ava to forgive me for being away for so long. It took quite a few walks and treats for Ava to become my special dog once again.

Chapter 30
Horse Racing Jobs

Lesson: If you feel like having a tantrum. Take a deep breath. This inconvenience is only a small part of your life.

Soon, I was back on the casual work bandwagon, and continued on to do some work for the horse racing industry.

I only work once a year for the Cox Plate, and the Melbourne Cup carnival. The days are long, and often I am on my feet for long periods of time. Sometimes it can be hard when you have to talk to thousands of people during these events, but I enjoy the interaction of being in the customer service industry. All I have to do is provide instructions to locations around the racecourse. I find it funny when the ladies are so dressed up and beautiful in the morning, then later in the afternoon, these same ladies have makeup running down their faces and are carrying their high heels because it is simply too painful to move. Some of the ladies are very smart, they carry ballet flats in their carry bags. And you can tell the difference, even though the material of the ballet flats is rather flimsy, you are still protected from the ground which may be sticky with beer or full of other nasty things. I love the men that are hired by the racing club, who walk around with their bag of helpful items such as a simple Band-aid, which can provide relief to someone who is suffering from a blister, or a nice dash of perfume to make the day a little bit brighter. I think that's the best thing about working for a huge company, they look at the little things that can make or break a day of a customer.

Working at these big races means that security is very intense. Every day you have to be scanned by security wand, go through metal detectors, and have your bags checked. It can be annoying, but this process makes me feel safe and secure in the knowledge that no one can sneak anything lethal into the premises.

There was one time while I was working at the gates, scanning tickets, and this staff member had a big tantrum. She was frustrated after missing the bus, and now she had to go through security checks. She told security that she was a staff member, and that her little bag does not contain any bombs. She dumped all the contents of her bag onto the floor, yelling, 'See? No freaking bombs.' The police moved fast and restrained her. Our team leader had to call her boss to see where to go from here. It is not often that we have to restrain our own staff members. Her boss said because of her bad behaviour, she would not work the carnival; we can't have people be that angry, working front of house. After being notified that she wouldn't be working the Cup Carnival, the staff member started crying and said she was sorry. But it was too late, security had to escort her back to the bus. She would be spending the rest of the day regretting her bad behaviour.

Working in the customer service industry can be tough. It can be both good and bad. You have to be flexible, and read a situation so you can act accordingly. Working in the customer service industry for so long has made me into such a versatile employee. I'm good in any situation and can handle most things.

Chapter 31
Recruitment Agency Work
Lesson: Find joy in the small things.
Surround yourself with friends who care about you.

The football and racing season were coming to a close, and I needed to find some more work, so I ended up working for recruitment agency.

They needed people to work for the transport industry, to assist with bus replacements, so I decided to try out for the interview. I ended up travelling to their head office, which was a two-hour journey. When I first knocked on the door of the office, I could see people just staring at me. No one made a move to open the door. It was very strange, there was no receptionist to greet you, just a bunch of people sitting down. Eventually, someone opened the door, saying I had to call the agency. Then shut the door on me. I was standing outside fuming. Eventually someone came out and I pushed past him. There was no way I was not going to attend this interview, I had travelled for so long. I sat down and glared at the person who had shut the door on me. She looked down. And I had a silent victory in my head, no one was going to deny me this interview!

Eventually, someone came out of the back room and explained what the position with the transport organisation would involve. She told us to fill in some forms, and soon we would have a one-on-one interview.

It was an easy interview, all I had to do is chat about my customer service work and why I wanted to work for the recruitment agency. I simply said I enjoy working with a variety of customers from all over the world. I just love the diversity of being surrounded by people from all around the world, bonded by their need to include public transport in their day.

Needless to say, I got the job, and went on to travel all around Victoria assisting with bus replacements. What I loved about working on behalf of the transport organisation was that this was an opportunity to discover areas of Victoria that I would otherwise would never think to visit. One of these areas was Broadmeadows. While it was a tough area, I loved chatting with the older locals who just wanted a chin-wag and someone to chat to. There was this older Italian gentleman who never failed to make me laugh. He had all these corny jokes ready for every day I was there.

It sounds silly, but when I worked at Hallam Station, I fell in love with the toilet music. The music was so catchy that I found myself singing the tunes while waiting for passengers to direct to their appropriate buses. It was somewhat awkward working at Hallam, as the bus stop was close to a sex shop. I could see the types of people that went into the store. I was surprised that they looked like everyday people, and at one point, I even saw a family go into the sex store.

When the recruitment agency discovered I was good on the microphone, every day felt like I was a famous speaker. But in reality, all I was doing was telling the passengers what bus to catch to the city, or the bus that would take them in the opposite direction.

Sometimes when people looked at us, it seemed like we were just on our phones all the time. But in reality, there is an app which shows us when the next bus is arriving, or we have to communicate in group chat with our team leaders, who have to document our role to our main client.

It made me so sad when someone decided to capture one of our team members on his phone, and decided to comment, 'Who else wants this job doing nothing?' This person posted this photo on social media, and it had well over 50 comments of people either agreeing or disagreeing with the photo. I was disappointed and scared that people would take a photo of me, and take it out of context, for all the world to see. We worked in rain and sunshine, with sometimes over 10 hours on our feet. This was not easy work, and we had to make sure we gave great customer service as well ensuring we were up to date with any changes in transport. While it looked like we were on cruise control, we were really working hard, so that people could get transport home or to work in time.

Through the recruitment agency, I got to work special events, which were really fun to be involved with. I loved working for the Melbourne Cup Parade, AFL Parade and the New Year's Celebrations.

Working for the New Year's Celebration was a great highlight. Every year, I avoid the city because of the crowds, but for once I decided that I didn't have any plans, so I might as well work and earn some good money.

We started at 5 pm, before the major crowds, and it was pretty easy. All we had to do was walk up and down, answering any questions about the fireworks and facilities. People were in good spirits, and were eager to count down to 2020.

It was a really nice atmosphere; people had come prepared and brought in rugs and picnic baskets full of yummy food to share.

I was even impressed with the portable toilets. Usually, I'm tentative about using these facilities, as they are often very dirty. But the City of Melbourne hired great cleaners, who made sure the toilets were bearable.

Soon it came down to counting down the minutes until the new year began. When it hit midnight, we started to see fireworks beginning from Marvel Stadium, which made the city look magical, bathed in many colours.

People were standing with big smiles on their faces, watching the fireworks, and it was so wonderful to see the joy that simple fireworks brought to people.

It really had not dawned on me that it was 2020. I wasn't out celebrating with friends, I was working, surrounded by many strangers.

When it was 2 am, it was time to clock off. I was glad I was with my friend Bec, who had worked with me. We gathered a few of our new friends, and started to walk to the station together for security. I felt much safer.

Just before we arrived at Southern Cross Station, we saw a big brawl on the bridge. It was scary to see. There were groups of young men yelling at each other. Some were throwing punches and jumping on each other.

At that moment I felt so frightened, I had never seen so much hatred and violence in one go. I was happy that I was with a group of people, and that we protected each other. When I reached Southern Cross Station, I was so happy to be safe and sound.

When we boarded the train to Flinders Street Station to transfer to our line, it was a nice ride. But when we approached Flinders Street Station, we saw this huge crowd of people on the platform. We were surrounded by so much hate and anger. I was scared to get off the train. The doors opened and instead of letting us pass, the crowd on the platform pushed their way in. There was no respect for letting others out. One guy trying to get out punched another guy pushing his way in. I was afraid it was going to become another brawl, but luckily this moment didn't turn out to be a fight. We eventually made our way onto the platform, and jumped on the train home.

I had decided for safety that I would drive my friend Bec home. We eventually arrived at the station where my car was parked. Surprisingly, for 5 am with no sleep, I was wide awake and able to drive. We decided to make a pit stop at McDonalds for a McChicken Meal with a Diet Coke. This was my first meal for 2020! Nothing beats McChicken!

I eventually drove home and had a shower, then prepared my room to sleep. Going to bed at 6 am reminded me of shift work. You have to make sure your room is prepped for sleep in the daytime. I sprayed lavender and made sure my room was dark, and eventually slept until 2 pm. It was like jet lag, but without travelling anywhere exciting.

I really enjoyed working for the recruitment agency, but the thing with temporary employment is that one moment you could have plenty of work, the next minute you're begging for work. I needed a job that I could depend on.

Chapter 32
Home and Community Care

Lesson: Be open to help. Sometimes we let our pride get in our way. And that can make life more difficult than it needs to be.

I had missed working with seniors in the community, so I decided to work for an agency that assists in helping clean houses. They were short shifts, ranging from 1.5 hours to 2 hours, but these houses were close to home. It wasn't much of a hassle to go from one house to another.

One of my favourite clients was Ellen, she was full of life and always had a smile on her face. She was so organised, with all her cleaning products shown neatly in the laundry, which made my role easier. All I really had to do was vacuum the house, clean the bathroom and do some general dusting and wiping.

She loved to have a chat about her outings at the RSL, and her husband who had passed away. She talked fondly of her dog, who used to love to sit at her feet while she watched her favourite TV shows.

Every time that I arrived, she told me to acknowledge the Queen, who was in the calendar on proud display in the kitchen. It was Ellen's ambition to reach 100 years old and receive a letter from the Queen.

One of Ellen's greatest fears was going into a nursing home. She talked about her friend who had moved into a nursing home, how it was like her life had been sucked away. Her friend missed everyday life, and the simple freedom of turning the key into her own home: a home that she had spent a lifetime in, rearing her children and being with her husband.

It was Ellen's fear of losing her independence that kept her strong. There was a stage where she had trouble washing her body in her shower. Even though she struggled, she was adamant that while she could, she would keep going. But then, she said if she needed help down the line, she would be open to getting it.

Her daughter took her to the nursing home to have a look, and Ellen said it looked ok, but didn't want to go. One step into that nursing home was like God's waiting room, she said. 'One minute you're there, the next minute you're in heaven.' Her greatest fear was letting go of independence, and depending on others to live day-to-day.

She loved where she lived, as this was her home, and so close to everything. Within minutes she could go to the doctor's or the shops. It was the perfect location.

She also loved her neighbours. She said they looked after each other, and they always popped in for a chat. She never felt lonely, and also looked forward to visits from her daughter and grandchildren.

Often while I was cleaning, she would enjoy having a chat. Or if she wanted to watch her favourite show, she would put the radio on for me, so I would not get bored. If I had missed a spot, she was quick to tell me! Especially in the bathroom, with all the little cracks!

Once when I had finished cleaning, I had found her sound asleep in her comfy chair. She had dozed off to the Million Dollar Minute show, so I had decided to hover above her whispering her name, hoping that would wake her up so I could get her to sign my paperwork. After almost five minutes of whispering her name, I gave up. I could still see her breathing, so she was still alive. I didn't want to give her a heart attack, just to wake her up. So, I decided to sit down and watch the Million Dollar Minute show. It was really nice; it was such a hot day and she had air conditioning. Twenty minutes later, she woke up and saw me sitting down, watching the show. She apologised and I said, 'No worries. I was enjoying the show, it is so addicting!'

She laughed. She said, 'Now you addicted, you can't stop!'

Another client, Nadine, lived so close to the beach. She was in such a prime location that often she would get real estate agents asking if she would be interested in selling her property. One of these agents called her house and she got so angry she started yelling into the phone, 'What? I can't hear you! I can't understand you', and hung up. She said the real estate agents were like hyenas, waiting to jump on their prey, and she would not have any of it. This was her home, and this is where she would stay. What was really sad was the back room was full of clutter, it was like being on the set of hoarders. She had two washing machines, and lots of boxes full of stuff cluttering her rooms. I was scared I was going to trip, but I was intrigued by a portrait of her mother at the very end of the room. It was such a beautiful, intricate portrait of her mother at a young age, and I could see Nadine reflected in her. I could have just imagined what Nadine would have been at a young age, feisty and full of zest.

What was really sad was that she had not been in her backyard for years. She depended on her son to mow the lawns and do general maintenance. When I washed her blankets, she had mastered a way to hang these blankets in her laundry. There was a clothes horse in her backyard, where these blankets would have become dry in an hour. She was too scared to go into the backyard, where there was potential to trip.

She had an emergency alarm pendant which, if pressed, she would get assistance, but she felt too proud to wear it. I asked why she didn't wear it, she said it was like admitting she needed help, and she didn't.

Nadine did not own any cleaning products. I had to use an old vacuum which was manufactured in the 1970s. After cleaning the main areas, I had to empty the vacuum cleaner, and I could not find the opening to empty the vacuum. I eventually, after much looking, found the opening, and within seconds all the dust went flying everywhere! Including my face and hair. I looked like I had been battling the dust monsters and lost.

She also provided vinegar to clean and sanitise her bathroom. It was weird to not use any modern cleaning products, but her preference was an all-natural approach. She wanted to leave the world as naturally as possible, and that went down to her cleaning products as well!

She looked forward to trips to Aldi with her son. It was so funny, the excitement she got from a bargain. She said she was a convert, and that she would never go back to the big guys, Woolworths and Coles, while putting the cans into her pantry. I loved her passion and her belief in standing up for herself. Her body may have been frail, but her personality was powerful she would not look down on herself, but went full pelt ahead with her values.

When I left the agency, I was sad to leave my clients. They will never know how much I admired them. I learnt so much from them, and the things I learned from them will always make my world a little bit brighter.

Chapter 33
Call Centre Life

**Lesson: Praise good customer service.
You can make someone's day so much brighter!**

I looked up jobs in call centres and ended up working for an agency that worked within the government.

At the time, I was also pitching a workshop to a retirement home which would involve residents sharing their story with local students.

It was hard to choose between them both, but I decided to postpone working with the retirement home to pursue the government agency work.

I realised if I wanted to move forward with my dreams that I needed funding, and a full-time job would solve this issue. I could still do what I wanted to, but have a stable job to catch me if I fall.

I put the workshop on the back burner, and joined the government agency. There was so much training involved, we had two weeks in the classroom and two weeks on the phones. It was pretty intense to be back in the classroom again from 8.30 am – 4 pm, sometimes I had to catch myself from falling asleep. It was pretty hard, jamming so much information into my brain, and now looking back on it, I don't use half the things they talked about. When it came to week three, I was pretty nervous about going on the phones.

Being on the phones wasn't too bad. Once you got comfortable with your product knowledge and how to handle calls, the role became easier. However, the type of customers could be full on. Some customers just wanted to yell and rant. That could be hard, especially if they didn't give you the opportunity to help them from the start. Sometimes they were so angry about waiting on the line for a long time, they built up so much frustration. Once they got through to me, often, they forgot they were speaking to a person, and wanted to spill all their rage into me. I had no chance to calm them down or just focus on what exactly they needed help with. One caller started yelling after I said, 'Hello, how can I help you?' I tried to calm her down and said, 'Ok, can we just focus on how I can help you today, so we can get this done and you can move forward with better things?' That calmed her down for a little bit, and I managed to sort out her issue. Then she started to yell again about losing her job, and how it was so hard to get through to a person. No matter what I said, nothing could calm her down. After five minutes of yelling, she demanded that she speak to my team leader. It took a while to get my team leader to assist, and by that stage I imagined the customer would be red with rage. After 10 minutes, my team leader was free. There was literally nothing else my team leader could have done to calm the customer. When a person is so deep in rage, it can be hard to see sense. Nothing that could be said or done could please that person. After five minutes, my team leader explained that all the customer had done since she commenced the call was yell abuse, and that was not acceptable. My team leader said, 'Thank you for your call', and hung up.

After that phone call, I realised I was not a punching bag for verbal abuse, and if I had done all that I could to assist, then there would be nothing else I could do. Now, if a customer becomes verbally abusive, I know I can safely say, 'Thank you for your call, this call has been terminated. Goodbye.'

Others were calm, and just wanted a simple hand. I loved listening to the diversity of different people from around Australia, especially Indigenous cultures. It is like a different world. I soon got used to being described as someone from the white mob, and hearing cultural ceremonies in the background.

Sometimes, it was hard being on the phones. I started out as being open to trusting people, but then ended up being wary of what was being said. People will do anything to receive money, and even lie about not completing certain activities to achieve the terms of their payments. Working in this call centre initially was difficult, there was so much focus on achieving good statistics that great customer service didn't even register. That was so disappointing, because the ability to listen and react accordingly should be at the heart of every conversation. Every customer service position I've held in the past has celebrated my ability to provide that sense of empathy and can-do attitude. I had to evolve and begin to reduce this experience, in line with the organisation's short call policy. Do what need to be done and fast, and not 'over-servicing' the customer, as they put it.

Working at the call centre wasn't all doom and gloom, I did enjoy chatting to customers and helping to make their day a little bit brighter. Even if we had to keep a tight eye on achieving key performance indicators, I hope my personality made a little impact in their world.

One phone call that I fondly remember was with this elderly gentleman. He had problems with the online self-service platform. He was 80 years old, and I was impressed that he had made it so far online. He had issues with gaining access to his online account and didn't want to bother his grandchildren for help, so he decided to speak to a real person from the helpline. It took a while for him to gain access to his account, but he was so proud that he eventually got the services he required linked up. He told me that it took him hours to get this up and going. He was so proud that he had gotten so far. He had taught himself the basics of how to use the computer, and had faced so many barriers to get to this stage. His experience showed me if you persist, you will eventually get where you need to be. And that you can use the computer at any age, you have just got to be willing to try.

Sometimes people forget to praise good service. And often, you don't expect people to provide good feedback on their experience with you. I was taken by surprise by one caller. I had assisted her to gain access to her account and had given her good tips on how to gain the services she required. She told me that often people don't go too much into depth into what goes wrong, and that she appreciated all my advice. She went on to tell me that she had made a new year's resolution to praise any good service she gets within the year. She said people often are first to say something bad and complain, but never think to provide feedback on the people that work hard to provide exceptional service. She said, 'It is people like you that make it easier for people like me.' We want good service, and people that care. I was having a pretty crappy day until her phone call, and she made me smile for the rest of the day. Sometimes it's the little things that make a difference.

I have good friends at the call centre, who make coming into work a little bit better. I am grateful for this job, as being in this role enabled me to work on two books. Also, to be able to get these books published in the real world. I honestly believe all these casual jobs came into my life for a reason: to provide a way to make my dreams a reality, and to meet people who I otherwise would never become good friends with.

After a few months at the call centre, I was able to organise leave on Wednesdays, so I could conduct the workshop with both the seniors and young students at the retirement village. The first session I conducted went really well, but it was up to me to talk about workshop fees and it was pretty awkward.

When I chatted to the leisure coordinator, she said the families may be able to come in and observe the session. However, being on a Wednesday, it was difficult. I did chat about a small fee for my expertise and materials.

I felt bad asking for a fee, and the residents were not happy with paying the $20 for the eight-week workshop. The fee was more directed to their families, so they could enjoy their grandparents' story for many years to come. I thought, maybe I can volunteer my time for this one session instead, and ended up creating an activity which involved the young students asking questions and interacting with the seniors. The topic was school, and was devised as an ice-breaker for both generations.

At first the students were a bit nervous, but they started to warm up and get to know each other. And that made me happy to see the potential of this workshop in bringing together two vastly different generations.

I realised while I loved working with the students and seniors, I was doing too much, and it was starting to get to me.

You can only do so much before your body starts to break down, and say, I've had enough; you need a break. At the time, I was working seven days a week, I was simply aching to have some time to myself, just to stop rushing from job to job. After much thinking, I decided to stop doing the workshops, and just focus on working at the call centre to make my goal of publishing my first book possible.

Chapter 34
Working During Coronavirus – Public Transport
Lesson: Wear bright colours. Be a little silly. Make someone smile

While most people during this time had to stay at home, I was one of the many essential workers that needed to travel to a workplace. I worked in a call centre that involved working with lots of private information that couldn't be shared with the public.

My world hadn't changed that much, except I no longer worked weekends at my event roles, which I missed so much. I loved the diversity of these different workplaces, and being surrounded by customers who were excited to see a concert or a football match during the AFL season.

Working during this time could be so hard. I had to double-think every action I made, and always make sure I was very hygienic. Before Coronavirus, I had used hand sanitiser, but not all the time. Now, every time I touched something, I had to think about the germs that might be attached to that item, and ensure that I had my hand sanitiser to clear away harmful bugs. Every time I caught the bus in the morning, I had to be sure that I kept my social distance. Even though I tried, sometimes it could be hard to do. Some people don't care. Even if the bus had enough room to space out, they decided to sit in the seat in front or behind me. And if they coughed, I got scared. What happened if they had Coronavirus and they were spreading the virus around? That one cough could be deadly or send me to hospital.

Every moment I was aware of, and I wished I could just switch off and not care. I wanted to believe the world was normal again, but it would never be the same. Every time a huge group of people jumped on the bus, I was frightened, especially if they looked rough and were swearing their heads off. One time, at the very start of the Coronavirus pandemic, I was wearing both a mask and gloves. These passengers had just come from McDonalds, they were eating food and blaring their music loud. One of the passengers looked at me and said, 'F&%ken bitch has a mask and gloves. It is not that bad.'

In that moment I felt scared that she would spit in my face. But she continued laughing with her friends, and eventually got off the bus. After then, I was grateful that I didn't have any other passengers abuse me because of my protective gear. Everyone has the right to feel safe, and not be abused because of their choice to protect themselves.

In saying that, I had some characters at the Dandenong Station pass me by. They made me smile. That station attracts some interesting people with loud outfits. Nearly every afternoon, this man on a bike passed through. He wore the loudest outfits, from every colour under the rainbow. I think he commuted to the local supermarket on the train just for fun. After a hard day at work, where I had to be so serious, I took solace in enjoying his crazy green clothing, or his cartoon character outfits, like his Pokémon onesie.

I hadn't seen him before the Coronavirus pandemic, so maybe that was his intention: in a world that had been taken over by all these restrictions, there should be a glimmer of fun and light. Maybe when the world returns to normal, I will wear Pokémon colours to celebrate the freedom to do the things I took for granted, such as sitting down to enjoy a coffee with friends at my favourite store.

Sometimes I missed the regular characters, such as this man who I think worked in construction. Every afternoon, he jumped on the bus and when he sat down, he opens his legs wide. I swear he was trying to social distance before it became the regular thing to do.

Every time someone sat next to him, he would let rip a massive, giant fart. I would laugh on the inside when the passenger next to him started to twitch their nose, and look around for any empty seat away from him. And when someone departed their seat, the passenger would make a mad dash away from him. I nicknamed this man 'the Farting Man', and I was grateful that he made me laugh on the inside so much. Thank you, Farting Man, for your comedic service. You will never know how much you have brightened my day.

Chapter 35
Working During Coronavirus
Lesson: Don't be a squirrel hording nuts. Money comes and goes. We can only work so much before we break down.

Every day I woke up and I had to mentally prepare myself for the day at the call centre. Some days it felt like the world was erupting around me. I had customers who were in so much pain. When they came through to me, the first thing they wanted to do was abuse me and tell me off for their long wait on the phones. While I understand waiting for long periods of time can be frustrating, there is no point yelling at the person who you have waited so long to speak to. When you build up so much anger, it can be hard to help you and get to the heart of assisting with the problem. Sometimes I had customers who were so appreciative of the work that I did, and that made the day easier to get through. I had one customer where the phone was disconnected twice, and she had every reason to be angry. But when she got through to me, she was so happy to just get through to a person. It was a simple enquiry, but the work that I did made her day so much easier. She was now able to complete her application and get on with her day. I felt so appreciative of how nice she was, and grateful that she had decided to take a deep breath and just be polite.

For me, working 30 hours a week was enough. Even though while I was at work I didn't feel so mentally stretched, on the weekends I felt very drained. Some of my colleagues were working up to 50 hours a week. One of my workmates that I chatted to in the tearoom said I should take advantage of all these extra hours, because when this was all over, we would be back to reduced hours. She reminded me of a squirrel, hoarding nuts for a rainy day.

You never know, with casual work, what you are going to get. While I understand this mentality, I honestly believe you need a life outside the call centre.

Sure, we don't know what is around the corner. But we only live life once. Enjoy some of those moments with your loved ones. Take advantage of long walks. Look after your mental health. We only have one body and one brain. Money comes and goes. You don't want to wake and realise that you spent most of your time at work.

Sometimes, on my time off, it could be hard to wake up in the mornings. My body just felt so incredibly tired. Talking to people non-stop, for sometimes up to 12 hours, can take a huge toll on your mental health. Sometimes all I had the energy to do was take my dog for a walk and enjoy a long round of Netflix. Sometimes it hurts to care so much, and have so many emotions surrounding you on a weekly basis. I know what I did was important work, but sometimes I wished I had chosen a more light-hearted profession, where I could be creative and make people laugh. We all make our own impact on the world, and I hope what I have achieved at the call centre made it easier for people to live during this crisis. Those calls were important. And I hope that my personality makes an impact on their world.

Chapter 36
Impact of Coronavirus

Lesson: Your mind can only retain so much information. Try to learn in small chunks. That's the best way.

There were days where there were bumper-to-bumper calls. Some of the calls were easy, others hard. We had many customers calling because they were struggling due to the Coronavirus.

For some people, it was really hard to make that initial phone call. Their pride often resulted in huge sighs and arguments. They had waited a long time to speak to me, and they were quick to point out that they had waited hours. Sometimes, even though I had answered their question sufficiently, they wanted to stay more on the line to make their time waiting on the phone more worth it. For others, they looked on the bright side. They knew what they had to do, and if they needed a little help, they would take it.

We were crash-trained to perform activities enabling us to help our new customers. I felt vital in the process of keeping the Australian economy going, so one day all these customers could go back to their jobs, doing what they did well.

Then, after a few weeks, suddenly our calls stopped pouring in. We often had 5 to 20 minutes of waiting time in between calls. While it was a relief to not be talking non-stop, I felt suspicious. Surely in amongst this crisis, people had not stopped asking for help. I wanted to assist, but I felt hopeless, and that I was no longer an essential worker.

Our company started asking us to leave early every day, there was not much demand for phone customer service and they were eager to save money. While it was nice to leave early, I was worried, *Has my job become obsolete?* What was going on?

Some staff got phone calls even before they started, telling them to not come in. Some staff did not receive this call, and rocked up to work, only to be told their shift had been cancelled. Soon, the staff moral in the call centre started to shift towards the worst. We were all concerned about what was happening, and if our jobs would be on the chopping block.

The demand for phone calls had made our company create another call centre on the other side of Melbourne. They had fast tracked equipment, such as headsets, so that 400 new staff members could take calls, leaving us in the lurch. All our calls were being redirected, leaving us with very little work. Our company decided to train all their customer service staff at our branch in processing, which was behind the scenes work, dealing with assets and figures stuff that was beyond our heads. This was a role that we didn't apply for, but if we wanted to stay employed, we had no choice. It was either processing, or you leave. The first round of 100 employees were trained in a room that was boiling hot. It was hard to take in new information, and some employees ended up crying in the bathrooms, when they could not work out how to calculate figures. Others had enough, and by day two had quit. This training was beyond their expertise. They did not apply for such an analytical role. After the first batch were trained, it was time for my turn. I had seen the impact on the first training group, and I was not looking forward to becoming a figures person. I am the type of person that fell asleep in maths class, or doodled in the margins of my exercise book when it came to algebra.

My expertise was talking to people and then figuring out how to help, not looking at assets paperwork and deciding what to do from there.

I was fortunate. My group only had 50 people, and was conducted in the smaller part of the call centre where it wasn't too hot. Our trainer had a lot of personality, she had bright red hair and had a lot of gusto. She worked long hours, and after training us from 8 am to 4 pm, she had another shift working as team leader for the processing staff until 11 pm. She had a lot on her plate, but plenty of energy to try and get us to learn these new skills. While I was appreciative of her loud personality, it was just too much training jammed into one week. There were times where I doubted my abilities, and just wanted to crawl into a corner and cry. This was not the role I had applied for; my background was in customer service, and I felt stupid. I wanted to leave, but I persevered in the hope that I would do well in this role.

While in training, an email popped up, congratulating our manager for a good job in getting the Melbourne branch up and going. I felt betrayed, like we were not good enough, and what we had achieved over the past year was not appreciated. It was not fair that they changed our role and others got to do the job that we had applied for in the very beginning. One of my colleagues told me that I looked so sad and confused. I realised my face expressed my sadness in a way other people could see. Usually my personality is so bright and bubbly, but I had turned dark. I had become unhappy in a role that no longer suited me. I had one more week, which involved training live with assistance. This week would be the factor that would see me either stay or go.

Chapter 37
Processing Life
**Lesson: Don't be hard on yourself.
To learn a new skill will take time.**

Our one week of processing with assistance loomed up. I was not looking forward to this week, which would see all my training used in the live environment. I was nervous, I had this power to go through records and make changes, which I felt I was not equipped to do.

I felt like I was literally faking being competent but, on the inside, I did not feel qualified in a role that had changed so much. Those six days of training did not fill me with confidence. I had spent most of the week confused and worried that I was no longer able to do my job well.

Our trainer kept telling us she was not worried, and we were all doing a good job. I felt like she had to be worried. We did not know what we were doing, and it felt like at nearly every single step I had to ask for help. I did not feel independent in my role, more like a panda that just wanted to fall asleep consistently. Looking at all these computer screens made me sleepy, especially not really knowing what direction to take.

Day one, I was stuck on an activity all day. I was confused about what steps to take. For every activity we had to read blueprints which showed you, step-by-step, what to do. But sometimes it was so confusing. Often, I thought I was on the right track but then found out I was reading the wrong blueprint. I felt like a dog chasing their tail. I kept imagining the customer getting frustrated with me and my abilities to do the job. But of course, the customer had no idea what I was doing and there was no need to be hard on myself.

I literally felt like a bad detective, trying to understand what exactly I needed to do. When I needed help, I had to put a flag up to be in the large queue for floor walkers, who were able to assist with the next steps. It was draining, waiting, and I felt sorry for the floor walkers, who literally had most of our group of 50 people waiting for assistance. From a group that hardly needed any help to now a huge group needing help, it was such a huge change. We were no longer independent, and needed guidance at nearly every step.

I was told to look at guides that showed, step-by-step, how to do activities, but the issue was that these guides were not well written. I spent hours trying to decipher what to do, with every step showing me to another guide, which did not answer my question. I literally banged my head on the computer. How could I help the customer, if I was confused about what exactly I needed to do? I was not analytical, and felt like all my skills and knowledge were going down the drain. I told myself to take a deep breath, they couldn't fire me if everyone around me were having the same issues.

I was talking to my colleague, who was so excited to be rostered on the phones, but then they had changed her role back to processing the next day. She told me she was so frustrated, and could not understand why the company hated her so much, to tease her with telephone work then switch her role back to processing.

I had to call a customer to ask her to upload documents, which was not too bad. I was nervous. Her husband had passed away a few months ago. When I called her, she said, 'This is not usual, this is not normal for you to call.' I said that perfectly fine, and if she wanted me to send a letter instead it was ok. There was no need for this phone call to continue if she was worried about security. After that, she did end up saying yes, and I was able to ask her the questions that I needed to in order to move forward with the conversation. She ended up crying when I had to ask personal questions, but it was ok. This phone call was most likely an emotional release for her. I felt bad, but then I thought, this role was important as she needed assistance badly and to get that help, she needed to know what exact documents she needed to upload.

While I don't feel like I am doing well in this new role, it is those phone calls that make the job worthwhile. I like that I am helping those in the community live the best life they can.

Our company knows there is a lot of bad morale in this call centre, so they are constantly thinking of ways to make their employees happy, such as holding a processing graduation party with free cake and sandwiches. But I have a feeling the company needs to do more than that. The company needs to put us back on the phones in a role that everyone can thrive well in.

I will stay in this job as long as I can bear it. All these hours at the call centre enable me to save for my next dream, to publish this book. If you have a goal, it makes it easier to stay in a bad workplace. But I don't recommend staying in a job just for the money. At times, it feels like my soul is breaking just a little bit. I need to be in a role where my personality thrives.

Chapter 38
Post-Covid Public Transport

Lesson: Be mindful of others. Swearing will only make people uncomfortable. Respect will take you many places.

When the first wave of Coronavirus restrictions started to lift, more people started getting back to everyday life. This meant that workplaces were gradually re-opening, and people needed to get to work by public transport. While these were great economic impacts, this meant bus journeys became busy again. I was used to having a whole row of seats to myself, and being able to social distance. Now, I was lucky to have a seat to myself and not have someone coughing my way.

People started to embrace freedom, and with that, gradually the buses became crowded. Some passengers were not even tapping their Myki card for their journey, and pushing their way on the bus.

It seemed like the world was gradually becoming normal, and I was afraid of the aftermath of all these people together in the one bus.

I slowly become aware of every little cough, and disliked Fridays, when from 4 pm, people would start drinking alcohol and playing loud music on the bus. People didn't care that others were on the bus with them, their behaviour showing disrespect to the bus driver who was taking them on the journey. It was their life, and they didn't give a f&%k.

Gradually, some of my favourite characters boarded the bus. Farting Man was back, legs spread wide, daring anyone to sit next to him. He was trying to social distance, and was succeeding in scaring people away from him with his loud and deadly farts. I was happy he was back, he still makes me smile.

However, some of the tougher characters also boarded the bus, and sometimes I had to look away from them. I'm not sure, but they seem to have a lot of anger inside and they just want to create fights. If I hear the words, 'What are you looking at', I dread that something horrible will occur or pray that we are close to McDonalds where they usually jump off for a meal. Usually, I hear conversations where I wish there was an undercover police officer nearby, some of these conversations can contain so much swearing. They just don't care who eardrops on their conversations.

I think they had a long way to go to make public transport safe, particularly during this time. There needed to be regular cleans and inspectors on the bus

I hoped that the compulsory masks would help. It didn't feel like the end of Coronavirus, and we all needed to make sure that we were still being vigilant, to keep each other safe. If you didn't need to take the bus to work, it was better to stay at home where you were safe.

Chapter 39
The Second Wave

**Lesson: Embrace your own community.
Smile and wave. Make people feel less lonely.**

We had a little break from restrictions before the second wave of Coronavirus hit in July. We were back on level three restrictions, where we were allowed to go to work, but only go outside for four purposes: work, exercise, medical and caregiving reasons, and for essentials like the groceries.

I felt disappointed. It was so nice to have the freedom to go into a coffee shop, and just enjoy socialising with friends in a public environment. I was grateful that I took the time to complete a First Aid course during that time, and have simple drinks with friends. It was those little things that I learned to cherish the most.

This time, everything was taken seriously. It was now compulsory to wear masks everywhere, even outside exercising with the dog. If you didn't comply, you received a massive fine. It was so strange, going into my call centre job with the mask still on. And then, exposing my ear to get a temperature check. If my temperature was too high, then I would not be allowed into the workplace. At the start of stage three, we had an employee try to sneak in. He had COVID 19, but was most likely anxious about providing for his family, so he decided to go into work anyway. Luckily, he was stopped before he went into the office. At that time, we did not have pandemic pay, so if working at the call centre was your only job, you would end up with no work to support your family. What was concerning, at the start of the second round, was that there was no social distancing, so if someone had the virus it would easily spread around the call centre. And this proved to be true, with our other branches having to shut down because employees had Coronavirus.

A temperature check can only do so much. A person with Coronavirus can walk around and not realise they have the virus until they start to display the symptoms.

The call centre, at this time, decided to take on new recruits for the telephone role. While having a peek inside the training room, I was shocked that there was no social distancing. People were literally standing so close to each other, looking at screens. I felt really anxious, looking in and thinking of another potential break-out, simply because the call centre decided to not take social distancing seriously.

Soon the union took action, and forced the call centre to take social distancing seriously. It took a while, but eventually there was only one person per pod. Usually we had three people in a pod, which included three chairs and three computers. While I was grateful for this change, it felt strange. Even though I was surrounded by people, I felt lonely. I missed the fun banter of my colleagues, and simply seeing a smile. Our faces were all covered up, and I felt like I was isolated. I just stared at the computer and worked, occasionally popping my head out of the pod to look out the window.

With the majority of seats taken away, soon shifts started to get cancelled. Priority went towards those that were on full-time contracts. It felt like the workforce was divided between casuals and contractors. But in saying that, even if you were on contract, your shifts would get cancelled. There was no stability either way. I'm not sure what the future holds for this call centre job. But for now, I just have to wait and see what the future has in store.

Chapter 40
Entrepreneurs: Generations Apart
Lesson: Slow down and focus on what you need to do. With every step you can make your goal a reality.

Way back in 2012, I had created a magazine full of the stories that I had gathered about seniors in my local area. It was such a huge process, getting all the stories together for publication and I had learned so much. I wasn't too sure if I would make another publication, as it was a lot of work.

In 2019, I decided I was ready to create another publication: a book, titled *Entrepreneurs: Generations Apart*.

Entrepreneurs: Generations Apart made me slow down and focus on what I needed to do, to make my goal of being a successful speaker and writer a reality. I wanted to learn from people who were doing what makes them happy every day.

Over the year, I had interviewed entrepreneurs under 30 and over 60, out of a simple curiosity: what makes people drop everything and follow their dreams? I fell in love with each interview. I thought it would be amazing to have all these interviews in one book for many generations to enjoy, and be inspired to take a chance on their big ideas. I thought it would be easy just copy and paste everything into one document, but it was much harder than that! When you have 51 entrepreneurs, it takes a lot of organisation. This is especially true when you are publishing a book that has the potential to sell copies worldwide. I had to make sure everyone signed permission forms, and that the photos provided were suitable for publication. I had to chase people up for high resolution photos. And of course, working with entrepreneurs meant that it was highly possible that the business they created from day one would evolve into something else! In some cases, I had to stalk LinkedIn profiles and Instagram accounts to get their contact details. I was dedicated to making this book happen, and at times I thought I never would.

I was lucky to partner with Sarah from Malvolio Designs, and she helped to craft the book, from inside my mind, into reality. I also needed help from a publisher to place *Entrepreneurs: Generations Apart* on the Ingram Spark platform, so that the book could be sold through Amazon.

The book took a few months from the final draft to become a reality, and it was amazing to finally hold the book in my hands. To feel and hold a publication that started as an idea was such an amazing experience. I am still amazed to see that the hard copy of *Entrepreneurs: Generations Apart* exists, to be celebrated for years to come.

I believe that sometimes you have jump off the beaten track to create a path that only you can travel. The road may be full of bumps, but it is one that only you can pursue, and enjoy the journey along the way.

I am a casual job-a-holic, and I am proud to be one.

www.ingramcontent.com/pod-product-compliance
Lightning Source LLC
Chambersburg PA
CBHW070306010526
44107CB00056B/2504